Reflections of
ISAAC WOLFE
BERNHEIM

Copyright © 2016 by Bernheim Arboretum and Research Forest

All rights reserved.

No part of this book may be reproduced or transmitted in any form or by any means, electronic or mechanical, including photocopying or recording, or by any information storage and retrieval system, without permission in writing from Bernheim Arboretum and Research Forest or its assigns.

ISBN 978-1-941953-34-1

Printed in the United States of America

Reflections of Isaac Wolfe Bernheim is a collection of material from two books Isaac Wolfe Bernheim authored about his life, one published in 1910 and the other published in 1929.

The Story of the Bernheim Family, by Isaac Wolfe Bernheim, was previously published by
JOHN P. MORTON & COMPANY
INCORPORATED
LOUISVILLE, KENTUCKY
1910

The Closing Chapters of a Busy Life, by Isaac Wolfe Bernheim, was previously published by
WELCH-HAFFNER PRINTING CO.
DENVER, COLORADO, U.S.A.
DECEMBER 1929

Reflections of Isaac Wolfe Bernheim was produced and republished by
Bernheim Arboretum and Research Forest, in partnership with:

Butler Books
P.O. Box 7311
Louisville, KY 40257
phone: 502-897-9393
fax: 502-897-9797
www.butlerbooks.com

REFLECTIONS OF ISAAC WOLFE BERNHEIM

In April of 1867, Isaac Wolfe Bernheim arrived in New York City, an 18-year-old boy with a few years' work experience, grandiose hopes for the future, and little else. After sixty years of hard work and a successful career in the distilling business, he left 14,000 acres of land, now known as Bernheim Arboretum and Research Forest, "for the people of Kentucky, and their friends, as a place to further their love of the beautiful in nature and in art."

Republished, here, are two autobiographical reflections Mr. Bernheim made on his life, one published in 1910 and the other published in 1929. Understanding Mr. Bernheim's personal history, his outlook on life, and his perspective on social responsibility, gives us a much deeper understanding and a better appreciation of the wonderful legacy he left us.

THE STORY
OF THE
BERNHEIM
FAMILY

ISAAC WOLFE BERNHEIM

Previously Published by
JOHN P. MORTON & COMPANY
INCORPORATED
LOUISVILLE, KENTUCKY
1910

———— TO THE MEMORY OF ————

MY MOTHER

From whose high faith, spiritual courage, and saintly sacrifice
I first drew the inspiration and ideals that have enabled me
to combat the world, I dedicate this history
in grateful and affectionate devotion.

And Cain went out from the presence of the Lord,
and dwelt in the land of Nod, on the east of Eden.
And Cain knew his wife; and she conceived, and bore Enoch;
and he built a city, and called the name of the city
after the name of his son, Enoch.
And unto Enoch was born Irad; and Irad begat Mehujael:
and Mehujael begat Methushael: and Methushael begat Lamech.
And Lamech took unto him two wives:
the name of the one was Adah,
and the name of the other Zillah

GENESIS 4: 16-19.

I make this quotation from the Holy Book to show that even in the earliest history of Man there was a well-defined ambition to maintain the integrity of descent. It has ever been thus. The pride of lineage is universal, and is attractive alike to priest and to layman. But in a democracy, my own feeling is that lineage should yield to achievement, for history is, after all, simply the biography of man's accomplishment.

It has come to be a widespread practice in our country for people of means to nurture their family trees. When the past does not produce them naturally, it is not difficult to procure whole forests. The professional provider of ancestry does a thriving business. I have neither the need nor the intention to enlist his offices.

My sole purpose in preparing this little book is to present a history of the Bernheim Family in general and that of Isaac Wolfe Bernheim's in particular. It is for private circulation, and therefore I have dealt with intimate things. I have adhered strictly to facts, and if statements are made that may grate harshly upon the ears of some Bernheim of a future generation, let there be palliation for this in my well-known innate sense of fairness and truth and my abhorrence of all that is false and hypocritical.

What follows is but a tiny rivulet in the mighty stream of Jewish narrative. The histories of many Jewish families are part of a larger story, wherein Romance blends with Tragedy in a great race-epic. The Jew, master of the Ages, has made his triumphant way through the travail of persecution and the throes of martyrdom to a mighty place in world power, and I am proud and glad that the record of my family should take its place in Hebraic annals.

The Jew was so long on the defensive that no opportunity was given him for the preparation of those family records which reveal so intimately the character of any people. Realizing the lack of such literature, I have ventured to write this modest volume in the hope that the Bernheims of tomorrow may find something of profit in the chronicle of their kinsman of today.

I. W. B.

CONTENTS

PART I
THE STORY OF THE BERNHEIM FAMILY

The Name Bernheim 1
My Parents 5
My Childhood 9
My Boyhood Days 15
My First Employment 17
I Land in New York 25
My Start in Business 29
I Begin My Life in Kentucky 33
My Friend Elbridge Palmer 41
Our Business Career 45
New Blood in the Business 51
My Sons 53
The Bernheim Distilling Company 61
The Romance of My Youth 63
My Mother 69
My Wife 71
My Politics and Religion 73
My Brother 77

PART II
THE GIFT OF THE JEFFERSON MONUMENT

The Offer and Acceptance 83
The Commercial Club's Tribute 91
The Dedication 97

PART III
APPENDIX

Advocate Temperance 107
New Building 111
Banqueted 115
Work of a Year 116
Deal Closed 120
I. W. Bernheim, Distiller 121
Give Bonds 123
Planned Home of Hebrew Congregations 127
Trustees for a Commission 129
Guiding Maxims 131

THE STORY OF THE BERNHEIM FAMILY

THE NAME BERNHEIM

THE name Bernheim, meaning Berne-homer or Bern-home, is undoubtedly of German origin. It is derived from the city of Berne, which in the Fourteenth Century formed part of the German-speaking section of what is now Switzerland, and which had harbored for many generations a large and prosperous settlement of Jews.

In the year 1348, the tales concerning the poisoning of the brooks and wells by Jews first found credence in the southern part of France, where the Black Death at that time had obtained many victims. In a certain town of southern France, one day in the middle of May, 1348, the whole Jewish Congregation, including men, women, and children, together with their holy writings, were cast into the flames.

From that place the slaughter spread from country to country until it reached Berne, where the annihilation of the Jews on the charge of poisoning was systematically carried out. The consuls of Berne, according to Gratz's History of the Jews, were particularly active in this persecution. They addressed letters to Basle, Freiburg, Strasbourg, Cologne and many other places, stating that the Jews had been found guilty of the crimes charged to them.

It would indeed be interesting to follow the history of these unfortunate victims of a blind hate in their wanderings, but poverty and insecurity of life gave them neither time nor inclination to engage in historic work. Suffice to say, that my great-grandfather, Loeb Bernheim, well known in Schmieheim as "Loebele of Thiengen," emigrated during the middle part of the Eighteenth Century from Switzerland to Schmieheim, a small village in the southern part of the Grand Duchy of Baden, and it is in that poor but hospitable village that the writer of this history first saw the light of day.

My grandfather, Solomon Bernheim, born in 1772, was the youngest of the four sons of Loeb Bernheim, all of whom lived and died in Schmieheim. The Jew, in the Eighteenth Century, had neither rights nor privileges save such as were purchased for money or were given to him as matter of favor or charity. He was forbidden by law to own real estate of any kind, yet he was forced to pay taxes. He had no voice in the management of the affairs of the municipality, and could hold no office. Despite these deprivations, he was impressed for military duty, but could not even become a corporal. In his attempt to eke out a miserable existence, he could follow only the vocation of peddler or trader, middleman or broker.

It was not until the latter part of the Eighteenth Century, when the liberating spirit of the French Revolution began to spread its enlightening and generous rays even into the most remote recesses of Germany, that the Jew was treated more humanely and his circle of activity became somewhat larger. He was then allowed to become a merchant, to learn a trade, to follow some of the professions, notably those of lawyer and doctor, and to become an owner of land.

My grandfather, Solomon Bernheim, who had lived under these unfortunate restrictions that beset his people, was a soldier in the great Napoleon's army. He was a courier, and served with credit. On his discharge he followed the occupation of itinerant merchant, and as a side issue handled old iron, rags, beeswax, and similar products in Waldkirch, a town about twenty miles distant from Schmieheim.

Well do I remember him. He was a man of medium size, well knit and sinewy, with finely developed features, broad forehead, and bushy white hair. He had an intensely religious nature, and was devout in the performance of his religious duties. He was equally upright in his home life. His wife, Ella Schnurman, was also a native of Schmieheim. She is said to have been one of those sympathetic yet strong women who have ever been the refuge and preserver of Israel.

Out in the open a Jew might and did suffer abuse, contumely, and derision, experience all kinds of disappointments, make sacrifices innumerable in order to earn enough to hold body and soul together. Yet in his home he would always find that tender sympathy, that peculiar spiritual encouragement, and above all that loyal affection from wife and children which steeled him to new endeavors and made him proof against all temptations. Such was the wife of my grandfather—a veritable mother in Israel! They raised a family of seven children, comprising five daughters and two sons, of which the older, Leon Solomon Bernheim, was my sainted father. He was born in Schmieheim on September 19, 1808.

My grandfather remained poor because of the expense of raising a large family. He was a firm believer in the value of a thorough education. Both my father and his brother, my uncle Henry Bernheim, who emigrated to the United States in 1850 and who died about 1878 in Selins Grove, Penn., where he was a merchant, received their education first in the Hebrew School at Schmieheim and later in a small graded school at Ettenheim, about four American miles from Schmieheim.

In those days a man, in order to become a licensed merchant, had to pass an examination, before a regularly constituted official board, in German, correspondence, bookkeeping, and kindred subjects. In fact, no one was permitted to engage in commercial pursuits without first having successfully passed such an examination.

My father received his license as merchant and was the first Jew to open a regular store in his native town. His commercial career was, considering the unsatisfactory conditions, a fairly creditable one. The first fruits of his labor went toward the support of his immediate family. Then as now, in Europe, it was imperative that each marriageable daughter be provided with a dowry of a certain sum in cash, together with an outfit of linens and other articles with which to start a household. Imagine the task of my father!

He provided outfits and dowries for five sisters, purchased a modest home for his aged father, and then, after all these obligations had been performed, began to consider seriously his own happiness. As the head of a mercantile establishment, blessed with what was in those days considered a liberal competency, and above all, endowed with physical attractions of no mean order, he was considered a great catch by the maidens of all the surrounding country towns. He was blonde, broad-shouldered, and stood over six feet in his stockings.

In the choice of a wife he did not look for money—rather for good family connections, education, and physical charms. He found all these qualities combined to a remarkable degree in the lovely person of Fanny Dreyfuss, from the neighboring town of Altdorf. She was recognized as the fairest girl in all that country, was eighteen years of age, and had a mind far above the average.

Her father, Rabbi Moses Baer Dreyfuss, was a merchant in Altdorf. He had far more interest in the study of the Bible, the Talmud, and other intellectual pursuits, than in his business, however, and consequently it did not prosper. Her mother, the daughter of the Reader of the Jewish Congregation of Altdorf, was a member of the village aristocracy, as rural aristocracy went in those days, and was an intellectual and influential force in the community.

Rabbi Dreyfuss died after a few years of happy married life, leaving three girls and two boys, one of whom, Mr. Samson Dreyfuss, is still living. He is a successful merchant, and occupies the highly respectable and much sought-after position of Town Councilor in Freiburg in Baden.

Another brother, Mr. Samuel Dreyfuss, emigrated to America about 1850, settling in Smithland, Livingston County, Kentucky, where he conducted a successful mercantile business until 1861. Then, broken in health, he returned to Freiburg in Baden, where he entered the wholesale notion business with his brother Samson. He died in 1896. One of the sisters, Miss Babette Dreyfuss, became the wife of M. Livingston, a well-to-do merchant of Paducah, Kentucky. She died in confinement, of nervous shock produced by the bombardment of Paducah by the Confederate forces under General Forrest in 1863.

The third sister, Miss Jeannette Dreyfuss, married Mr. Benjamin Weille, a respected merchant of Paducah, Kentucky, became the mother of an interesting family, and is, at this writing, still in the enjoyment of robust health.

MY PARENTS

My father was a progressive business man, and, as far as the law permitted, met with his full measure of success. He became the owner of a modest home which later on, by various additions, became next to the old castle, the tallest house in Schmieheim. He enlarged his business, became a wholesale buyer and seller of

LEON SOLOMON BERNHEIM,
I. W. BERNHEIM'S FATHER AT 34

wine, which was produced in large quantities in our community, and also became a land owner in a modest way.

At the time of his marriage my father was thirty-six. Next to the wife of the Rabbi, my mother quickly became "the first lady" in the Jewish community of Schmieheim. Attractive in person, she was no less attractive in fine qualities of mind and heart. She was well educated. After going through the village school, her father sent her to Strasbourg, which was then a part of France. Here she became proficient in the French language, as well as in the higher branches of housekeeping, such as sewing, embroidering, dressmaking, and millinery.

She was religious, but not bigoted, and to her credit be it recorded that she was the first woman in all that country brave enough to discard the old and hideous custom of concealing her hair after she entered the married state. This created a great commotion in Schmieheim, and it was more than a generation before the reform movement became general among the married women.

My mother was a reader of the best German literature, and being gifted with a fine memory she retained much that she read. She thus became an interesting conversationalist and a delightful correspondent. Her letters to me showed a graceful style, elegant diction, and often a depth of feeling and of thought that made them peculiarly charming.

With all these accomplishments, however, she remained a level-headed, practical woman, so that when, in 1850, my father's eyesight became defective, and when shortly afterward he became temporarily blind by reason of the formation of a cataract, she assumed control of the business and managed it with skill and ability for nearly two years. My father's sight was then restored by an operation of Professor Schelius of Heidelberg, who had then a worldwide reputation as an oculist.

Despite the disparity in the ages of my parents, their family life was always an ideally happy one, though it was interspersed with periods of great sorrow. The eldest child, Henry, a bright boy, died when he was about two years old. The second child, Rosalie, died in her babyhood. My father was devoted to his family and idolized his children.

A story told me on one of my visits to Schmieheim by an aunt, Mrs. Marie Rosenstiehl, now over eighty years old, clearly

FANNY BERNHEIM,
I. W. BERNHEIM'S MOTHER, IN 1884

illustrates his affection for his children. My parents visited a fair
in a neighboring village, leaving the children in charge of their
aunt. A servant was sent to the cellar to draw some wine for the
midday meal, and either through negligence or ignorance failed
to properly close the spigot. All the remaining wine leaked out.

The accident was discovered late in the afternoon by my aunt,
who, realizing the loss and feeling the weight of responsibility
for it, started on foot to meet my parents, so as to break the sad
news as gently as possible. My father perceived his sister from a
distance, and noting her excitement quickly rushed toward her.

"What is the trouble, Marie?" he asked. "What accident has

occurred? Are the children all right?"

"Yes," replied Marie, "your children are safe and sound, but a cask of wine has been lost during your absence."

"Never mind the wine as long as the children are all right," replied my father.

The loss, which was a serious one, was not mentioned again that evening.

My father gradually accumulated property. Prosperity sometimes makes people better, and in some instances it has the opposite effect. Frequently it produces increased avarice, breeds pride, and develops self-conceit. I am proud to say that prosperity made my father a truer, deeper, and more useful man. By nature broad-minded and big-hearted, his fortune, if fortune it can be called, made him all the more sympathetic toward the poor and needy and increased his influence for good in the small community.

He followed closely the Biblical injunctions as to charity. One tenth of whatever he raised in his fields, and one tenth of his profits in other pursuits, conscientiously went to the poor. The doors of his store were never closed to the needy when suffering for the necessaries of life.

In a small community almost evenly divided between Jew and Gentile, differences often arose which threatened to produce bitter feeling between them. My father on many such occasions acted as peacemaker. Although neither permitted to vote nor to hold office, he was often called into consultation about important matters by the Mayor and by the minor officials in the town.

At the very height of his greatest usefulness he was stricken with pneumonia, and, after an illness lasting but eight days, died on January 9, 1856, in his forty-eighth year. Besides his widow, who was just thirty, he left three children, and one yet unborn. I was the oldest, and had just passed my seventh year, having been born November 4, 1848.

MY CHILDHOOD

I am now in my sixtieth year. As I look backward over the stretch of my years, trying to figure out which particular period of my existence has been the happiest, I always arrive at the conclusion that it was the space of time between my birth and the death of my dear father. We children were idolized by our parents, our every want was gratified; we were indeed reared in the lap of luxury, as far as luxuries went in those days.

The death of my father brought about tremendous changes in our family affairs. The life of my mother, like that of her children; became from that time on and for years thereafter, one of trial and disappointment. The youngest of my brothers was born three months after the death of my father; he died in infancy. Another little brother, Karl, died shortly thereafter, in his second year. The old maxim that troubles never come singly was sadly verified in our case, and my mother suffered as it falls to the lot of few mortals to suffer.

The estate was ample to provide comfortably for us all, but it required careful attention and close application to details. Burdened with a family of small children and weighed down by sorrow, my mother was unable to devote the necessary time and attention to it. The absence of the beloved guiding hand in our family made itself felt more seriously as time rolled on.

It soon became evident that my good mother needed someone with experience to assume the management of our affairs, so as to conserve the estate. The guardian, a certain Mr. Uffenheimer, appointed by the authorities to look after the interests of the minor children, and who did his duty conscientiously, soon came to a similar conclusion. It was through his instrumentality, guided no doubt by the best intentions, that my mother was introduced to Mr. Louis Weil. The acquaintance soon ripened into mutual affection, and resulted in their marriage during the fall of 1857.

My stepfather, a man of middle age, slightly built, of dark complexion and of a somewhat bilious temperament, had some good qualities, and, like all mortals, some serious defects. He was above the average in intelligence, had traveled extensively, could speak the French language like a native, was an ardent lover of music and a violinist of no mean ability.

The simple life in a little village like Schmieheim, at the foot of the Black Forest, several miles away from a railroad and without a single social attraction, did not and could not appeal to such a man. Devoid of experience in the management of an estate, unwilling to adjust himself to the surrounding conditions, it soon became apparent that as a conserver of our estate he was a total failure.

He displayed little sympathy and still less patience in his intercourse with us children, which brought about early in my child-life a bitterness toward him which only years could soften and never completely erase. I was in my ninth year when he came into our life. I was a child, and by no means an angelic one, and I am willing to admit that I was not entirely blameless in the premises.

I was headstrong, and that weakness has accompanied me through life. Stubbornness and tenacity are twins, and they are responsible for much that is evidently bad and for more that may be found good and praiseworthy in my character. My mother shed many tears over the frequent quarrels between my stepfather and myself. The consciousness of having caused her so much unhappiness has been the source of bitter heartburning to me.

Though torn by the lack of harmony between her second husband and her children, she proved a dutiful and devoted wife to him. Two children sprang from this union—Herman, who lived for many years in Paducah, Kentucky, and who died in his thirty-seventh year while abroad in search of health, in his former home, Freiburg in Germany; and Sara, who married Mr. Samuel K. Cohn, and who resides at Cairo, Illinois, a happy wife and the mother of an interesting family.

I am proud to say that my mother, through her rare tact and good sense, raised these two children so that I always regarded and loved them as my real brother and sister. They in return showed a similar attachment and devotion to me.

But I am digressing. The temptation to put the cart before the horse comes to me at times with almost irresistible force, and when for the moment I yield, it is because my mind is untrained in literary work. Beyond writing occasionally a short article for a newspaper on some practical topic in which I may momentarily feel an interest, my literary activity has only extended to business correspondence in its various branches. In this particular line I have the reputation of being a master, and this quality no doubt came to me by inheritance from my mother, who, as I stated above, had an ability along such lines considerably above the average.

To return to Schmieheim, in the year of our Lord 1859, candor forces me to repeat that my stepfather was unsuccessful as a conserver of the assets of the family. He sold our acres piecemeal, and all the while the old business was ceasing to be profitable. To his credit let it be recorded that he made an honest effort to improve our financial condition by embarking in new ventures, all of which proved failures.

He engaged, for instance, in the manufacture of shoe-blacking. I well remember how, as little boys, my brother Bernard and I acted as assistants in his blacking factory, turning the crank that mixed the ingredients in a tub and afterward filling little boxes with the finished product. The enterprise was unsuccessful, because the blacking was unfit for use and therefore found no sale.

Later on, my stepfather took up the leather business and the handling of tools for shoemakers. This branch for awhile promised good results. Mr. Weil, however, was too easy in the extension of credit to the little shoemakers in the neighborhood, and made bad debts, which finally resulted in the total loss of the capital invested. The resources of our family had become well nigh exhausted by this time. There was nothing left save that part which was due us as minor children, and which was held as a separate estate.

All this happened in the years up to 1861, that memorable year in which the Jews in the Grand Duchy of Baden received their full civil liberties. Their emancipation was due largely to the act of the Grand Duke Frederick of Baden, as enlightened, liberal, unprejudiced, progressive, and humane a man as ever governed a people.

My co-religionists, for centuries half slave and half freeman, stepped quickly forth into the sunshine of freedom and wider activities. They were now allowed to vote and hold office in their respective communities. Cities and villages which had never extended the privilege of permanent residence to Jews opened wide their gates. Schmieheim, which was congested with Jews, felt itself relieved of its surplus population as if by magic. Many moved to the neighboring cities of Lahr, Offenburg, Haslach, and Karlsruhe.

My parents sold the old homestead and used the proceeds for the purchase of a small apartment house in Freiburg, which, in the light of later experience, proved one of the wisest acts of my stepfather. It was in the fall of 1861 that we went to live at Freiburg. The family at that time consisted of my parents, the author of this history, who was then about thirteen years of age, my brother Bernard, aged eleven, my sister Elise, aged five, my half-brother Herman and his sister Sara, who was then a baby.

My stepfather engaged in different pursuits, with more or less success. After a struggle of two more years his health was undermined and he was forced to relinquish all business activity. He became a prisoner in his room for most of the time. My mother furnished a few rooms, which were rented to students and actors. The income from these provided our scanty means of support. To fill the cup of sorrow to the brim, my sister Elise, to whom my mother was deeply attached, died after an illness of less than two weeks, in the winter of 1862.

My brother Bernard and I were thus the only children left of the first marriage. Both of us have every reason to be thankful, for we are still in the enjoyment of good health and we have been blessed with more than a fair share of everything that makes for happiness. The years that have intervened since that day have been strenuous ones for us both, and now as I retraverse the forty years in which we have worked together, I realize anew the value of our comradeship.

The prototype of our father, big-framed and big-hearted, content always to follow where I led, only putting on the brakes and opening the safety valve when I put on too much steam, always the same indulgent brother, never the censor, ever the man of peace and of affection, Bernard has been indeed a power and a blessing.

However, I shall proceed to the period of my boyhood days.

THE OLD HOMESTEAD AT SCHMIEHEIM, BADEN,
GERMANY, WHERE THE AUTHOR WAS BORN
NOVEMBER 4, 1848

MY BOYHOOD DAYS

The history of any boy raised by parents of scanty means reads about the same the world over. He is sent to school at an early age, and is taken out of school to earn a livelihood as soon thereafter as possible. I was sent to the village school when I was five years of age. The three "Rs" were taught by a rather strict teacher, who was a firm believer in the rule of "spare the rod and spoil the child." I cannot claim ever to have been bright at school. Everything that I learned came to me by hard work, but I had a great advantage in that when once a thing had entered my hard head it remained there for good.

When I was ten years old I entered a graded school at Ettenheim, a village about four miles from my home. This daily walk of eight miles, minus overcoat or underclothing, in severe winter weather was often a hardship, but I stood it for three years, and I attribute my hardy constitution largely to this hard physical experience.

In the fall of 1861 my parents decided that their means were too scanty to permit of any further extension of my education. I was therefore apprenticed to a commercial house, where I served for three years, in order to lay the foundation for a commercial career. I worked hard and received no compensation. These were indeed years of privation.

My business master was Johann Baptist Fischer of Freiburg. He was exceedingly strict in discipline and intensely conscientious as an instructor. The first year I served in the capacity of porter. I opened and swept the store, dusted the stock, and delivered bundles. The second year I received practical instructions in the selling of goods, and the third year I was initiated into the science of bookkeeping, correspondence, and the handling of money.

The duties of an apprentice, under such a strict master as it was my good fortune to have, were rather exacting. Still, in my third year I managed to earn enough money by outside office work at nights and on Sundays to pay for my clothing and other incidentals.

My term of apprenticeship ended on the 29th of November, 1864. I was sixteen years old. My good mother (blessed be her memory!) had made many sacrifices, depriving herself oftentimes of the very necessaries of life and cheerfully surrendering many comforts in order to prepare me to meet the responsibilities and requirements of earning my own living.

The boy of sixteen had gained experiences and received impressions which seldom are crowded into the life of one so young. Candor forces me to say that, unlike the experiences of the average boy, mine were not of a character calculated to make me look back gratefully upon that period of my life or wish to live it over again. They taught me, however, to love work, to practice economy, and to be self-reliant.

To these three qualities, coupled with my inherent abhorrence of things that are vicious and bad, I trace that limited measure of success that came to me in after years. These qualities will make the successful man in any walk of life and in almost any part of the world, and I would strongly impress it on my children, and on those who come after them, to acquire and practice them. Industry, economy, self-reliance, good morals—these are the foundation stones on which success is built. Without them sooner or later must inevitably come either disappointment, failure, or dishonor.

Robust health is not to be underestimated as one of the elements of success. It may fairly be assumed, however, that whoever leads a correct and moral life, likewise obtains a strong physical endowment. However, I am digressing again, and this time on morals. I certainly was not cut out for a philosopher or a poet. To me a thing appeals most strongly when I can feel it or see it, and always has. I will therefore revert to my text, and tell about the period of my young manhood.

MY FIRST EMPLOYMENT

Through the influence of my stepfather and with the active cooperation of Mr. Fischer, who furnished me with an excellent recommendation, I succeeded in securing employment as clerk with a firm in Mannheim. My first salary amounted to twenty-five gulden per month, which when converted into American money was about eleven dollars. When it is considered that out of this sum I had to pay board, lodging, and washing, and had to supply other little necessaries besides furnishing my clothes, it requires no mathematician to figure out that, even with the then proverbial cheapness of commodities in Germany, it required genuine financial skill to make both ends meet. The job itself was a hard and an exceedingly unpleasant one. I therefore resolved to make a change at the earliest possible moment, though I was determined not to give up one situation until I had secured a more desirable one. The opportunity did not develop until the following August (1865), when I obtained a position with Gebrueder Elkan at Frankfurt-on-the-Main, wholesale dealers in knit goods, and at that time one of the leading firms in their line in that city.

My first appearance in the office of the firm left an indelible impression on my mind. My place was secured by correspondence, and my employers had never met me personally until I came to work. They expressed keen disappointment when they faced a rather undersized boy of barely seventeen. Usually young men of twenty had occupied places of that nature. When I came to present myself, Mr. Bernard Elkan looked me over and decided promptly that I was too young and too small for the job. My eloquence, however, got the better of his judgment, and I was set to work. This unusual condition drew the attention of the members of the firm to me, and on more than one occasion I was shown favors which proved unmistakably that I had their goodwill and confidence.

My salary was little more than what I had received in Mannheim, but the business was a very extensive one. I quickly reasoned that the chances for advancement were decidedly better. Besides, Frankfurt was then, and is today, the financial and commercial center of South Germany.

It was there that for the first time in my young life I formed delightful acquaintances and congenial friends. Moving heretofore in the narrow limits of provincial towns, the life in the larger city, together with the activity in a commercial firm whose trade extended all over Germany and to foreign countries, had its broadening influence and produced in me a feeling of contentment and a conviction that here I found my true sphere of usefulness. I determined to round off my career in Frankfurt.

Everything seemed to favor me except my income. It continued to be barely sufficient to meet my ever-increasing needs. Winter was now coming on and I needed an overcoat, though up to this time I had never felt the need of one. In Freiburg and Mannheim only the rich could afford such luxuries, but in my new surroundings the possession of an overcoat became necessary if I was to maintain a proper social standing. I was too proud and too sensible to appeal to my good mother for assistance. I knew she would deprive herself of necessaries rather than refuse me my request. I had my brother Bernard at home, who by this time earned some little money as clerk in a law office, but his meager wages were urgently needed to keep our mother and the family in comfort.

In my extremity I decided to eat only two meals a day, and I went to work without any breakfast for weeks. It went hard, because my digestive powers were excellent. But I had to have that overcoat. I owned a little silver watch, a gift from my sainted grandfather. It went to the pawnbroker. Still, I was short of the necessary means for the garment.

How I raised the remainder is best explained perhaps in a letter handed me on one of my visits to Europe in 1896 by the cousin to whom it was addressed, and who came to my relief. It is written in German, which, translated into English, reads as follows:

FRANKFURT, NOVEMBER 12, 1865.

Dear Aunt and Cousins:
I am in receipt of your letter of the 9th inst., and beg
your pardon for my apparent neglect in acknowledging
your remittance of twenty-five gulden. In doing this
now, I beg to thank you for your kind and prompt
assistance. I should be only too willing to pay you this
loan back right now but for the fact that my cash on
hand is totally exhausted because of the purchase of an
overcoat costing thirty-five gulden. I expect to receive
the second quarter of my salary by the end of January,
and will by that time without fail pay you, etc., etc.

I was seventeen years of age when I became the owner of an
overcoat, and another year passed before I enjoyed the luxury
of a couple of suits of underwear. The fall and winter season in
our branch of trade was extraordinarily good. To keep up with
orders a great deal of night work became necessary. Early and
late I was on hand. When one or more of the clerks found it
convenient to excuse himself from night work, I was always
ready to do double duty. This pleased my employers so much
that I received a substantial gift in money before Christmas and
a respectable raise in salary by New Year (1866), even though
according to the custom in Germany, advances in salary were
not granted until the expiration of the full year. My work was
evidently appreciated, for I was entrusted with more important
tasks and was making rapid headway.

During the spring of 1866 war clouds began to appear on the
horizon. Bismarck had been for years perfecting the Prussian
army, and was making ready to force Austria into relinquishing
its further participation in the affairs of the rest of the German
States. War was declared during the early summer of 1866.
Frankfurt was very close to the scene of hostilities, and soon
felt its grim influence. Commerce stopped, business houses cut

down expenses and discharged employees by the wholesale.

My firm reduced its force to the minimum, fully three-fourths of our clerks losing their positions. A few, including myself, retained their places. I looked upon this as a mark of particular confidence and goodwill. I felt grateful to my firm, and was more than ever determined to show myself worthy of it.

In midsummer, while the battles of Langensalza and Aschaffenburg were being fought near Frankfurt, and while Prussia was concentrating her forces near the Bohemian frontier preparatory to striking the terrible blow at Sadowa which resulted in the dismemberment of Austria as a German State, there appeared in Frankfurt two Americans, who were forced to stop over because the railroad had for the time being discontinued its regular passenger service.

One of these, Mr. M. Livingston, an uncle by marriage, had spent some few days in Freiburg visiting relatives. He had called on my mother, and through her learned that I was employed as a clerk in a prominent house in Frankfurt. A stranger in a large city, anxious to meet someone who could help him to kill time pleasantly during his enforced idleness, he bethought himself of the nephew, and promptly hunted me up. It was—I remember it distinctly—a sultry afternoon when the American made his appearance at our place of business and asked for me.

A glance convinced me that before me stood a typical American. His broad-brimmed hat, square-toed boots, open face denoting democratic frankness and a rugged character, his plain, matter-of-fact, good-natured way—all attracted me immensely. I spent part of that day and the whole of the next day in the company of Mr. Livingston and his companion, who proved to be Mr. Moses Kahn, of Paducah, Kentucky.

Our conversation took a wide range. We discussed the war, argued about its causes and probable results, and made comparisons between things European and things American. I had never before come in contact with real Americans, and had not had the opportunity to get information at first hand as to business conditions, business opportunities, the mode of life,

I. W. BERNHEIM AT AGE EIGHTEEN

customs and system of government in their great country. I had read some books on America and had always been a great admirer of the republican form of government, but after all it was merely printed matter and consequently failed to make an impression. Here before me now were concrete examples of what America had done.

These two Americans, then both in the very prime of life, had left homes in Europe in their youth, poor in purse but rich in health and ambition, and had now returned on a visit, enjoying a degree of prosperity which only years of hard work extending over a lifetime and under the most favorable conditions could produce in Europe. It set me to thinking about my own future and what America could do for the young man with health, ambition, and a willingness to learn.

I had before me a life just beginning to become attractive from many points of view. I had behind me years of hardship and privation. My salary in another year would have afforded me not only a more comfortable existence, but also the enjoyment of modest pleasures. True, I was only a young clerk, but I was connected with a large firm, whose confidence I felt I had gained, and which promised a career for me such as was not open to many. Besides, Germany was the home of my parents and the land of my birth. Yet with all these advantages I realized that it meant the spending of the best years of my life before I could hope to carve out for myself an independent position, which at its best would yield only modest results in comparison to those which are to be attained in America with less effort.

My uncle was engaged at that time in the manufacture of cotton knitting yarn in New York. When I inquired of him what my chances might be in case I emigrated to America, he not only promised to give me a position in his office in that event, but agreed to lend me the necessary funds with which to pay my transportation to New York. Before we parted, when he resumed his voyage to Bingen-on-the-Rhine, where he wooed and won his second wife, I promised to leave for New York the following fall.

My fellow clerks, to whom I made known my determination to emigrate to America, tried to laugh me out of it. My dear mother, whom I immediately informed of my intention, would not listen to the idea and tried in every way to dissuade me from it, first by frightening me and later by appeals to my filial duties. My determination remained unshaken. My two uncles, Mr. Samuel Dreyfuss and Mr. Samson Dreyfuss, in Freiburg, were called in by my mother in her anxiety to induce me to change my mind, but to no avail.

Already as a child it was counted as one of my faults that I was headstrong. Later in life this quality developed into determination, and the trait has stuck to me up to this writing.

When once I had convinced myself of the correctness of a course, nothing but absolute failure would keep me from maintaining it.

The day for my departure had practically been set for the middle of October, 1866. I informed my firm in proper time of my plans. The senior of the firm, Mr. Bernard Elkan, who always had his watchful eye on me, received the information with great surprise, and in his fatherly way painted the dangers of the step. He dwelt on the promising future of my career in Germany, but my mind was made up and no arguments could induce me to alter my plans.

In the meanwhile the Prussian-Austrian War, which had lasted about ninety days, came to a close, and business quickly assumed an unwonted activity in Frankfurt. My employers asked me to remain with them a few weeks longer, which I readily consented to do. I was grateful for their interest, and despite the hard work had enjoyed my contact with them.

I left Frankfurt on the 8th day of September, 1866, and without solicitation received from my employers a few lines which I have always prized very highly. Translated into English, they read as follows:

> We hereby testify with pleasure that Mr. I. W. Bernheim served from August 26th of last year until today as clerk in our firm. During that time he proved not only a model of correctness, but by reason of his industry he deserves our special commendation. We can therefore cheerfully recommend Mr. Bernheim and tender him in his future endeavors our best wishes for his welfare and happiness.
>
> Frankfurt A. M., September 8, 1866.
>
> Signed   Gebrueder Elkan.

I returned to Freiburg on September 11, 1866, after an absence of nearly two years. My good mother, my brothers and my sister greeted me at the station, and it was a most happy reunion. My contact with the world had produced changes which my mother quickly noticed, and which gave her much pleasure. I had become polished, had better command of language, and because of the more fashionable cut of my clothes my physical appearance was greatly improved.

It was late before we retired that evening, and before I bade my mother "good-night" she had my promise to remain at home until the following spring. Always resourceful, she had already secured a clerkship for me with my uncles, Gebrueder Dreyfuss, for whom I worked from that time until I left for New York. The winter of 1866-1867 was a happy one. I had employment at remunerative wages, met many pleasant people in a social way, frequented the theater, took dancing lessons, and studied hard under an Englishman to become more proficient in the use of the English language.

I LAND IN NEW YORK

The seventeenth day of March, 1867, was an eventful one in my own history and in that of our little family. It dawned cold and dreary, and snow covered the ground. A carriage drove up to our humble home and took me to the depot. It was the first step in my long journey to the new country—America—haven of the hopes of millions of ambitious young Europeans.

For days before my departure my mother had been inconsolable. The occasion of my leave-taking was therefore a particularly sad one. Her grief was intense, and for the first time I almost regretted that I had determined to leave my native land. I soon recovered my composure, however. My brother Bernard accompanied me to the station, where we bade each other an affectionate "good-bye," little dreaming that in the course of a very few years he would follow to that Great Land of Promise which was destined to become the permanent home of all of us.

I traveled by rail to Mannheim, thence by boat down the beautiful Rhine to Cologne, whence, in company with many other emigrants, I proceeded to Bremen. On the 23d of March, 1867, we embarked at Bremerhafen on the steamer "Hansa" for New York.

The crowd on the steamer, recruited from all parts of Europe, was an interesting one. I soon found myself at home on the lower deck, and before long made some interesting acquaintances among my fellow passengers, and passed my time pleasantly. Some phases of life in the steerage did not appeal to me at all. Old and young, married and single, male and female, were all huddled together like so many cattle in illy ventilated, dark and filthy compartments, extending without a single partition the entire length of the ship. There was neither privacy nor comfort.

The food on the ship, which was abominable, was not set before the steerage passengers in a dining room. Space was too valuable for such conveniences. Each passenger was required to march to the kitchen with the necessary utensils, furnished by himself, to obtain his rations. If he wanted coffee he had to have a coffee pot, while for soup and meat he must have a tin bucket. The meat was unfit for a human stomach, and the coffee was made from chunks of German chicory. I managed to satisfy my hunger with large quantities of boiled Irish potatoes, which were quite palatable. As I had no special receptacle for these, I passed in my hat, which was filled brimful with the steaming tubers. The sea air increased my appetite wonderfully and I experienced little difficulty in eating daily a hatful of dry Irish potatoes, and thrived on the diet.

We came in sight of land on the 7th day of April, 1867. On the morning of the next day we were transferred to a small tug and landed at Castle Garden at noon. There we were met by United States officials, and each was required to state his name, date of birth, nativity, and give some other information. The commissioners were very particular in ascertaining the exact amount in cash each one of the passengers had in his possession. I answered all questions truthfully and correctly, and I am not ashamed to acknowledge to my posterity, as I did to the commissioner at that time, that besides some small German silver coins I was the possessor of twenty francs in gold, which is equal to about four dollars in American money. That was my state on arriving in America.

When the examination had been completed it was nearly five o'clock in the afternoon. Many of my fellow travelers preferred to remain overnight within the hospitable walls of Castle Garden (long ago put to other uses), taking their repose on the soft side of a wooden bench, which was furnished free of charge, rather than assume the risk of getting lost or robbed in a strange city.

My anxiety to find my relatives, and at the same time get away from the squalor in the Garden, induced me to set out at once. The factory owned by my uncles was situated on Spring Street, near Broadway. I struck out boldly, and after some inquiries here and there finally arrived in front of their place of business after dark. To my bitter disappointment I found the establishment dark and closed. I nearly fainted, for I was tired and hungry. A stranger in a strange land, I bethought myself of Castle Garden, the Asylum of the Emigrant. It was my only refuge, so I retraced my steps down Broadway and through the kindness of the gatekeeper—though it was against the rules—was again admitted. I spent the night, in company with many of my fellow passengers, on a wooden bench.

On the morning of the 9th of April, 1867, I once more emerged from Castle Garden. It was one of those sunny, bright, and pleasant mornings for which New York is famous. After securing breakfast and an American hair-cut and shampoo so as to look presentable, I turned my face up Broadway. The scene seemed completely changed. The evening before I had had no eyes for my surroundings, but was bent on reaching Spring Street to escape from my ill-smelling and uninviting surroundings.

But that fair morning I saw New York in all its splendor and glory. The bustle and activity on Broadway thrilled me, and the many signs bearing German-Jewish names all along the street instilled me with courage. I began to reason that if these firms, which were undoubtedly composed of men who like myself had once entered New York poor, had succeeded, why were not the same opportunities open to me? Early impressions are the lasting ones, and that beautiful, sun-lit April morning will be in my memory as long as life lasts.

I had no difficulty in finding the factory on Spring Street, but on my arrival another and a more serious disappointment awaited me. My uncle met me cordially enough, but I soon learned that his affairs were not as prosperous as he had left them the preceding summer when he started on his European journey. Raw cotton had declined rapidly, and in the spring of that year was sold in New York at eight cents a pound. In the preceding fall it had found a ready market at from twenty-four to twenty-eight cents in currency per pound. Those engaged in the cotton and kindred trades suffered greatly. The firm of M. Livingston & Co. had unfortunately anticipated their wants in raw cotton, and their losses brought them to the verge of bankruptcy. The factory had been idle for some weeks before my arrival. The depression in the cotton trade had its reflex in all other lines of business throughout the country.

My uncle, generous even under the most adverse circumstances, offered me his home as a temporary shelter, and made it pleasant for me. But he was unable to give or secure for me any employment. The country was emerging from a four year's civil war, and was in a state of transition. The war had produced an inflation of all prices; speculation was rampant, and finance generally was in a chaotic state because of the fluctuation in the currency. All these conditions produced a stagnation in the labor market, and the poor emigrants suffered.

My few francs were spent for car-fare in a daily search for labor. The outlook was becoming hopeless when one day my uncle received quite unexpectedly a visit from Mr. John Weil, an old schoolmate, who had a flourishing store in Wilkes-Barre, Penn. Mr. Weil was of a practical turn of mind, and after he had heard my story proposed that I should peddle goods in his section. He declared that when once I had familiarized myself with the language and customs of the country I would have no difficulty in securing pleasanter and more remunerative employment. I saw the point, and promptly acted on the suggestion.

On the following day my good uncle bought a box about two feet wide and three feet long, and had it filled with what were called "Yankee notions," consisting of needles, pins, spool thread, socks, suspenders, handkerchiefs, and ladies' stockings. He bought the goods for me on credit, guaranteeing the bill himself. On the 3d of May, 1867, I left New York in company with my newfound friend for Wilkes-Barre to start my career as a peddler.

MY START IN BUSINESS

I. W. BERNHEIM AS A PEDDLER IN
PENNSYLVANIA

Mr. Weil was correct in his prediction. The new avocation afforded me many opportunities to familiarize myself with the language and customs of the people and with the country itself as perhaps no other pursuit could. It developed me physically, and what was worth still more to me, it gave me a spirit of independence and self-reliance which stood me in good stead ever afterward.

If I were poetically inclined—and I now wish I possessed more of that delightful gift—how it would enable me to graphically and interestingly dwell on those days of wandering! I trudged along the peaceful Pennsylvania highways dreaming of future triumphs. Life glittered with golden promise of coming rise as a country storekeeper or of manorial affluence on a prosperous farm.

I liked the life in the open, and became so much attached to my travels that when Mr. Weil offered me a clerkship in his store during the summer I declined, preferring to be independent and to work out my own salvation in my own way. My affairs prospered from the very start, and my sales increased as I became acquainted. I worked conscientiously during the whole of that summer. Having accumulated some money, I decided to enlarge my business by carrying a more varied stock.

In October, 1867, I purchased a horse and wagon and went to New York to lay in a supply of such goods as I had heretofore handled. In addition I bought some clothing and other men's wear. My uncle, Mr. Weille, had in the meanwhile moved to New York from Paducah, Kentucky, and the two were kind enough to again secure a small line of credit for me.

I started out with high hopes, but soon discovered that I had made a serious blunder. To carry one's stock of goods boldly into a house and submit it for inspection to the prospective customer is a far easier proposition than to go empty-handed into the house, enumerate the articles which you have for sale, and try to receive permission to show your goods. In the former case a small sale could almost invariably be made, while in the latter procedure much valuable time was often lost in the attempt to get the customer into the mood to look at your wares.

Although the volume of my business increased, my expenses— especially the cost of keeping a horse—more than outbalanced my expanded earnings. My bills in New York began to mature, and though I financed as best I could, I soon convinced myself that my anxiety to increase my profits had gotten me into waters too deep for peace of mind. The month of November brought some relief. The Christmas trade was good, and once more I began to see prosperous times ahead of me. But my hopes were soon dashed to the ground.

The first snow of the season caught me with my outfit in the mountains of Bradford County. I had failed to make any provision for a winter's campaign, and was seriously handicapped. To carry on my business in that region required strong, sound horses and a good sleigh. My horse was poor and old and my wagon was light. To purchase a new outfit meant the investment of considerable capital, which I could not command.

I decided, therefore, to go into winter quarters, select some good neighborhood, and with the stock on hand open a store on a modest scale. I located in Overton, a little crossroad town in a then thinly populated section of Pennsylvania. I left my horse, which had become lame from heavy work, with a farmer by the name of Stroh, whom I knew to be a trustworthy man and in whose family I had often found a pleasant home. I remember well my friend's name, because unconsciously he is responsible for the complete change in my plans for the future, which resulted in the molding of my young life along different lines.

My business experience in Overton was not a satisfactory one from a money point of view, but socially it was a decided success. The young merchant with the store clothes and a prepossessing appearance had no difficulty in entering the select circles of Overton's best set. Parties where the young of both sexes met were of almost nightly occurrence, and I had a royal good time with these simple, rugged mountain folk. Some evenings were devoted entirely to dancing. Quadrilles or square dances, in which the figures were called out by the fiddler—we never had more than one musician—were danced exclusively. When one quadrille was finished you promptly took a partner for the next one. I introduced the German waltz, teaching some of my girl friends to dance it, and thereby strengthened my social position.

By way of a change, we had quilting parties, where the young ladies sewed bed quilts until the young men appeared, and then we spent the rest of the evening singing and playing games. There were also husking parties, where the young people shelled corn. When a quantity had been shelled, the corn was set aside and the evening spent in social intercourse. On Sundays I went to church and to Sunday school. I showed no preference for any particular sect, but was welcome in all the churches. My Sunday dinner was hardly ever taken in my regular boarding-house. Thus the winter passed congenially. By and by the snow disappeared, the air became balmier, Nature began to give signs of reawakening—spring was at hand.

My stock of goods was undiminished, and so were my debts in New York. I began to make plans for the coming year, and determined to take up my occupation of peddler with renewed vigor. I was in robust health, had read many books, had mastered the English language, and was therefore better equipped than ever before to be successful. I wrote to friend Stroh to send my horse and wagon to Overton.

While my letter was on its way I received a few lines from my uncles in New York, stating that their enterprise had ended in failure and that they had determined to wind it up and to return to their old home in Paducah, Kentucky, to open a retail store there. They offered me a position as clerk. The proposition did not appeal to me, and I was on the point of declining it when an answer from my friend Stroh arrived advising me of the death of my horse.

The death of that old broken-down nag quickly changed my plans. I accepted my uncles' offer. Pennsylvania thereby lost a peddler; Kentucky gained a young clerk. I disposed of my goods at private sale and at auction, wound up my affairs as speedily as possible, and on the fifth day of May, 1868, I was on the way to Paducah, richer in experience but poorer in purse than when I had landed in April of the previous year.

I BEGIN MY LIFE
IN KENTUCKY

In 1868 Paducah had no Eastern outlet by rail. I traveled in a roundabout way via Pittsburgh and Indianapolis to Cairo and thence by boat to Paducah, where I arrived early on the 7th day of May, 1868. It was a delightful, balmy morning, the kind that makes Kentucky peculiarly attractive at that time of the year. Before the stores opened I had occasion to take a walk around town, and I was favorably impressed with what I saw of the place. It was regularly laid out, had broad, well-kept gravel streets, and the stores as well as the residences gave the place a prosperous and friendly appearance. It was far ahead of Overton.

My good impression was increased as I came to know the open-hearted, warm and cordial character of the people. Kentuckians have their faults, but I felt then, as I do to this day, that the proverbial "Kentucky hospitality" is more than a meaningless phrase. The Kentucky greeting is spontaneous, and because of this spontaneity it is sincere and leaves a delightful impression on the stranger.

I met my uncle, Mr. Benjamin Weille, without delay, and was greeted most cordially by him and his wife—my mother's younger sister, whom I had seen when a child and whom I dimly remembered as a good-looking girl in Altdorf.

I quickly familiarized myself with my new duties. I swept the store and the pavement every day, kept the stock in good condition, and acted as bookkeeper and as second salesman. My senior was Joe Ullman, who in later years reached the goal of his ambition by becoming a member of the Paducah police force. Joe was a good salesman, and his services were particularly valuable because he had served as a soldier in the Confederate army throughout the war. He knew most of the farmers for miles around Paducah by their given names. In the spring and summer, when leaf tobacco was brought in from the surrounding counties of Crittenden, Livingston, Hickman, Ballard, and Fulton, Joe sold them their dry goods and clothing, swapped yarns with them about their experiences in the army, and sent them home rejoicing.

How I envied Joe, and wished I had been in the rebel army so that I too could shake hands with my old comrades, sell them goods and earn a good fat salary as he did! I tried hard to copy him, but never was a success as an imitator. As a result my usefulness as a salesman was greatly hampered. Although Joe was a kind-hearted fellow he was untutored and ignorant, yet he was a good salesman. I was an educated merchant, and I was a failure because I did not know the people and could not sell goods in the glib, free, and easy fashion required. My uncles, Mr. Livingston and Mr. Weille, were not much pleased with my services, and I realized that they had good cause for it.

In the August of that first year in Kentucky, one evening while I was busy with my books, Mr. Moses Bloom came in for a friendly visit. Paducah in those days was a good-sized village of from four to five thousand inhabitants. There was neither club nor theater. The town had a great many saloons, but it possessed only one beer hall where men could sit down and enjoy a drink in European fashion. The absence of suitable places where business men could meet socially to discuss the questions of the day was responsible for the prevailing custom of visiting each others' stores when the day's work had been ended.

Mr. Bloom was associated with Mr. Loeb in the wholesale liquor business, under the firm name of Loeb & Bloom. Both men were bachelors. Their store as a rule was closed quite early in the evening. With plenty of time at their command and no families to look after, they were frequent visitors at the different stores in the evenings. Their favorite resort was the store where I worked. I soon formed their acquaintance.

Mr. Bloom impressed me very favorably. He was then about forty years of age, of medium height, with very pleasing appearance and kindly ways. His polished manners showed that he had come in contact with good people. He had evidently received a fair German education, could read and write English fairly well, and was highly respected by everybody in the community.

Mr. Reuben Loeb was an entirely different personality. He was two or three years younger than Mr. Bloom, was tall and angular, sallow of complexion, and rather reserved in his ways. His education had been sadly neglected in his youth, for he wrote German badly and had not learned enough of the English language to read or even to write or speak it with any fluency. He was selfish and had enough cunning to make him a fair trader. Socially he was an undesirable companion, and I could never quite conceal my dislike for him.

On that particular August evening which proved so fateful to me, Mr. Bloom stood near the counter and watched me work on my books. He was evidently very much pleased, for he remarked in a careless, half-earnest, half-joking way:

"This boy would make a fine bookkeeper."

"Well," said my Uncle Livingston, who stood nearby, "you can have him if you like him."

A few days after this conversation Loeb & Bloom's so-called bookkeeper, a certain Mr. Cobb, who did not have enough clerical knowledge to tell a credit from a debit entry, was discharged, and I was engaged to take his place at a salary of $40.00 per month—in currency, which, according to its value then, was about equal to $26.00 or $28.00 in gold.

My employers were not mistaken in their estimate of my ability. I mastered the details of the business in a comparatively short time. I found the books in a deplorable state, and the work in the office, as well as that in the store, lacked any semblance of order or system. By degrees I reorganized the firm's business to the eminent satisfaction of Mr. Bloom, who was ever ready to commend my work and often expressed his pleasure and satisfaction.

My salary was raised from period to period, enabling me to replenish my wardrobe, which had become very shabby during my career as a peddler. It also permitted me to assist my good mother financially. By frugal living I was able further to save enough to pay my good uncles back the money which they had advanced for goods for my ill-starred Pennsylvania enterprise. It required more than two years of close economy to get out of debt, but I finally accomplished it. It is a source of pride to record the fact that I have never done any one out of a cent nor failed to meet any obligation at maturity.

As the years passed, my position in Paducah became an exceedingly pleasant one. I enjoyed the confidence of my employers, was in close touch with delightful friends and relatives, and I felt justified in looking to the future for still better things. I was inspired to greater effort by a statement of Mr. Bloom's that if I continued to give satisfaction he would in course of time give me an interest in the firm. This promise was made when I was barely twenty-one.

Late in 1869 the only drummer that our firm employed made one of his regular trips in West Tennessee, collected a considerable amount of money, and decamped for parts unknown, leaving a wife behind in Paducah. I promptly proposed to the firm that I take his place, and it was agreed that as soon as another bookkeeper could be found I was to become their representative on the road.

My brother Bernard was at that time a clerk in a lawyer's office in Freiburg. He had a very desirable place, yielding fair wages, and was well regarded by his employers. But his chances for advancement were exceedingly unpromising. To become a practitioner at the bar in Germany required a college education, which my brother unfortunately did not possess. He might after years of steady work have succeeded in obtaining a position as superintendent of the estate of some noble family, or if particularly lucky might have secured some minor position in the service of the State, but at best it meant a precarious livelihood. My mother had long since become convinced of the wisdom of my having come to America.

My brother had been kept advised of the improvement in

my material condition, and though never expressing in his letters a desire to look for better things in the New World, he became more favorably disposed toward America through the medium of our correspondence. When I informed him of the opportunity to become my successor as bookkeeper he promptly and unhesitatingly declared his willingness to accept the position. I showed his letter to my firm, and both members consented to give him the place if I would remain in the office long enough to "break him in." I readily agreed to do this.

Bernard reached Paducah during January, 1870. Two or three months were sufficient to fit him for the place, after which I went on the road. My mother's two older children were now in the United States, while she, with the two younger ones, remained in Germany. We wrote glowing letters to her, depicting America as seen by our young eyes. We were enthusiastic in our descriptions of its free institutions, and were ever expressing our confidence in our ability to carve out satisfactory careers for ourselves.

The Franco-German War came on in the summer of 1870. Both of us would have been in the army had we not in good time found homes in America. My mother then for the first time frankly acknowledged in her letters that she thanked God that we had emigrated, little thinking that in the space of a few short years she, too, would cross the ocean to join us on this side.

While Bernard developed into a finished bookkeeper, I, by hard work, built up a fairly satisfactory traveling business for the firm. Our salaries were raised from time to time, until in 1871 I earned $900.00 per year and my brother somewhat less. Our incomes permitted us to lighten the burden of the family in the old home and to lay something by for ourselves. In the meantime I continually kept in mind the promise of Mr. Bloom to give me an interest in the firm. It was early in the fall of 1871 that my brother and I decided to open negotiations with that end in view. Being the older and more experienced, I became the spokesman of the two prospective junior partners. I laid the matter before Mr. Bloom, but, aside from his promise to talk it over with Mr. Loeb, received but little encouragement.

I was not present at any of the conferences held by the two partners, but I have always suspected Mr. Loeb of being the one who put his veto on the proposition. Promised advances in salary were declined. My brother was asked to remain with the firm in the event I decided to sever my connection, but to his credit be it herewith recorded, it did not take him a second to turn down the overture. We would stay together or leave together.

The matter hung fire until Christmas of that year, when, after a final interview with Loeb & Bloom, in which the former became somewhat excited and abusive, we gave them notice that we would vacate our positions on the first of January, 1872.

Mr. Loeb was considered by those who knew him best as possessed of those peculiar instincts necessary for the successful detective. He was secretive, suspicious, and as cunning as he was ignorant. When we first broached the subject of obtaining an interest in the firm, he quickly concluded that someone else was trying to secure our services. He knew that the savings of Bernard and myself amounted to less than twelve hundred dollars, and that this sum was not sufficient to start a wholesale firm with, even on the most modest scale possible.

He did not find out until too late that we had made a friend in Mr. Elbridge Palmer, who had some spare cash and enough confidence in us to invest a couple of thousand dollars in our enterprise and to become our silent partner, should we decide to start business on our own account. To Mr. Palmer belongs the credit, and to him is due my profound gratitude as long as life lasts, for having made it possible for me to start out early in life in an independent way and to thus lay the foundation for whatever success I may have achieved in business.

Mr. Palmer and I had known each other for some years. When we first met he was a partner in the wholesale grocery firm of Palmer & Barber and I was the bookkeeper for Loeb & Bloom. Our firm occasionally bought groceries from them to fill orders, and they in turn purchased whisky from us to fill theirs. I made the monthly settlements between the two firms for my employers and Mr. Palmer for his firm. We were first thrown together in this way, and the acquaintance ripened by degrees into something akin to real friendship, if friendship it can be called, for Mr. Palmer was a most peculiar man. He spoke little, had but few associates, and was regarded by those who met him casually as a close-fisted man. He was careless in his dress, abstemious in his habits, and reserved in demeanor almost to the point of being a recluse. However, he was a close observer, and often remarked in after years that he had had his eye on me from the time I arrived in Paducah.

When negotiations for our admission to the firm of Loeb & Bloom had finally been broken off, I mentioned it to Mr. Palmer. At the same time I submitted our plans for the future. He listened to my statements, asked a few questions, and before we parted that night he had expressed his willingness to invest two thousand dollars in a wholesale liquor business, which, with our savings of nearly twelve hundred dollars, would give us a capital of about three thousand. We were to do business as Bernheim Brothers, Mr. Palmer remaining a silent partner, and receiving one third of the net profits of his investment.

The new firm started January 1, 1872, on an exceedingly modest scale, in the back part of a store on Market Street. Mr. Palmer, who had previously dissolved partnership with Mr. Barber, occupied the front part of the building as a wholesale grocery store. Bernard and I paid no rent and roomed over the store with Mr. Palmer, who at that time had no family, having been left a widower some years before. The firm thus unpretentiously begun has had an uninterrupted and honorable life to this day.

MY FRIEND
ELBRIDGE PALMER

Before proceeding to record the succeeding episodes in my life, I shall devote, in grateful remembrance, this space to my good friend, Elbridge Palmer, whose loyalty and confidence we retained up to the day of his death, which occurred July 3, 1896. His was, as I have said before, a peculiar nature. In fact, he often reminded me of a plant with an unattractive exterior which yet hid and nourished a sweet fruit within. His almost studious reserve concealed a tender and sympathetic heart.

When Mr. Palmer discontinued the grocery business he became cashier and later president of the City National Bank.

If the impecunious borrowers had been as close to Mr. Palmer and had known his generosity as well as I did, they would have broken the bank many a time. But that grave, silent man stood at his post, often hiding his real feelings and managing the affairs of the bank successfully. He made few friends, and kept strangers at a safe distance.

Our partnership continued for three years, and when we felt strong enough to acquire his interest he retired willingly, allowing us to repay his part of the investment, together with his share of the profits, in such easy installments as not to interfere with the growth of the firm. Our close relationship continued unchanged, while his confidence in our success, as well as in our integrity, became a sort of fixed religious belief with him. He gave us many evidences of his kindness and faith in us. As a banker he allowed us to borrow up to the fullest limit from his bank, and as an individual he endorsed our paper for any needed amount. The confidence shown by this taciturn and apparently immovable man can best be illustrated by the following incident:

My brother Bernard decided during the summer of 1882 to visit his old home in Germany. When informed of this intention Mr. Palmer had a sudden and unaccountable attack of the "wanderlust" and decided to join my brother on a visit to the "old country," as he was in the habit of calling Europe. The preparations were carefully arranged by Bernard. Mr. Palmer made no special effort to get ready. He simply packed an old oil-cloth valise, which had seen hard service during the Civil War, with a few belongings. All of these he religiously brought back, without the addition of a single item.

It is remote from my intention to convey the idea that he was unduly close or unreasonably careless in his attire. On the contrary, I merely wish to make it clear that he was always the same kindly man, simple in his habits and indifferent to the impression he created. At home or abroad, he lived his life on the theory that

"A man's a man for a' that."

While Mr. Palmer gave no thought to the personal preparations for his European trip, he did not ignore the financial requirements of our firm during his absence. He had kept in close touch with our affairs. He knew that during the summer months our financial demands were sometimes very urgent. Our business in those days was almost exclusively in the South, and collections were poor until the winter season, when the planters disposed of their cotton crops. On the day before his departure Mr. Palmer called at our office to make his good-bye call. While there he put his hand in his pocket, pulled out a piece of paper and handed it to me, saying:

"Ike, I am going away tomorrow with Bernard, to be absent three or four months. It occurred to me that you might require money which Charlie (Chas. E. Richardson, who was the cashier of the City National Bank of Paducah) might not be able to furnish. I have executed this note; fill it out with whatever amount you may need, and discount it in another bank in town."

Although spoken over twenty-five years ago, these words will always be fixed in my memory. Since then I have had a varied experience in trade and finance extending over many years, but in all that time I have never heard of a similar case of such absolute confidence in the integrity of a friend. In giving me that note, Mr. Palmer placed his entire fortune in my keeping. Had I been weak I might easily have brought about his financial ruin.

Our business, however, prospered while the two tourists were in foreign lands, and I had no occasion to fill out or discount the note. I had the satisfaction of handing it back to our benefactor upon his return, remarking that his act of confidence had touched me deeply and had made an impression which I would gratefully treasure as long as life lasted. In grateful remembrance of his kindness I named my youngest son, born in 1882, Elbridge Palmer Bernheim. I cannot refrain from expressing here the fervent wish that he may ever remember the debt his father owes to the man for whom he is named, and that he will always strive to be worthy of the loyalty that made it possible.

OUR BUSINESS CAREER

I shall proceed to sketch briefly the history of the firm which found its inception in the back room of a store on Market Street in Paducah, Kentucky, on the first of January, 1872. It might justly be claimed that the story is but a repetition of similar experiences of millions of enterprises which started in modest ways and by dint of persistent work and intelligently directed effort became big undertakings. However, this little history is written for home circulation, and for that reason alone I hope its recital may be found helpful and interesting to future generations of Bernheims as illustrating the fact that success comes as a reward only to those who in their youth lead moral and temperate lives. Such a course conserves vitality for the supreme struggle that is ever the forerunner of a real career.

College education to my mind is a luxury and not a necessity. When to health and a fair common-school education you add a good character and a determination to stick to a course once mapped out, the result spells "success."

I say it in all modesty and with no attempted self-praise that my brother and I were fully equipped to be successful. Our firm had no sooner started when we both settled down to hard, systematic work. For the first three years I did all the traveling for the house. After that period (and we had in the meanwhile passed successfully through the panic of 1873) our little capital had grown sufficiently to permit of an extension of trade, and my brother started to travel. Up to 1888 we continued as travelers for the firm, alternating on the work so that one of us was always at home. So faithfully was this order observed that whenever the turn of the one arrived to start out he went, regardless of whatever pleasures or family functions he must forego by reason of his absence from home. As an example, I might cite that my daughter Millie was born while I was on a business trip in November, 1884. The old motto, "business before pleasure," was never violated.

In 1875, after we had bought out the interest of Mr. Palmer, we admitted Mr. Nathan M. Uri as a partner. The firm name was changed to Bernheim Bros. & Uri, and the business was conducted under that name until 1889, when Mr. Uri withdrew voluntarily. We then resumed the old firm name of Bernheim Bros. As our capital increased we expanded, taking in more territory and engaging additional traveling men all the time. At the start we confined our business to a radius of about two hundred miles from Paducah. In fifteen years our trade extended over the entire South and into parts of the West and Northwest. The firm became the wonder and pride of Paducah.

It was soon evident that our business was outgrowing the town, which offered but meager facilities for the economical handling of men and merchandise in a big way, and that if its growth was to be maintained we must seek a larger field of activity. The prospect of leaving the place where I had made my start, where I had numerous friends and relatives, where I had found my good wife, where six of my children were born, and where my dear mother was comfortable and contented, was not pleasing. I had the proposition under advisement for over a year. I realized that a change meant greater business cares and also increased personal expense, and I further fully understood that the success or failure of the move rested entirely on my shoulders.

However, after we had taken an inventory in January, 1888, and discovered that our capital was growing by leaps and bounds, we decided definitely to seek a wider field of operation. Our choice fell on Louisville, which at that time was one of the great distributing centers of the country for fine whiskies. Accordingly our business and all of our belongings were transferred to the Kentucky metropolis on the first day of April, 1888. We secured a very commodious building on Main, between First and Second streets. The policy of increasing our trade with the increase of our capital was adhered to. We engaged more traveling men as we needed them, and soon our business extended from Maine to Texas and from New York to California. During 1895 we became the owners of the adjoining store.

Before we had settled on a plan for its improvement, however, an unfortunate accident occurred. Early in March, 1896, the bonded warehouses of the distilling plant at Pleasure Ridge Park, owned jointly by Block & Frank, Mr. Nathan F. Block, and ourselves, were destroyed by fire. The loss was covered by insurance, but the tax on the whisky, for which Mr. Nathan F. Block and I were sureties to the government, had to be paid. Our only hope of immunity lay with the Treasury Department, which had the power to abate it. The fire had started in the forenoon, on the roof of one of the warehouses and in plain view of the distillery and internal revenue employees. Its origin therefore could be accounted for easily.

The insurance companies settled the losses with reasonable promptness, but the government persistently declined to release us from our bond, which aggregated nearly a million of dollars. The Treasury officials even threatened to levy on the distillery and on my individual property. This jeopardized more than my entire fortune, and gave me many sleepless nights. We fought the case in Washington for nearly eighteen months, and finally succeeded in getting a cancellation of the bond from Lyman J. Grage, then Secretary of the Treasury, on the day before Thanksgiving, 1897. Hence we had immediate and definite cause to give thanks that year. During all the time that that calamity menaced we kept our courage and carried on our business with energy and confidence.

A modern distillery became a necessity as our affairs developed. As soon as practicable after the fire we had plans drawn for a plant capable of supplying our wants, and which was to be owned entirely by us. On the day after the election of our martyred President, William McKinley, in November, 1896, we began digging the foundation for this plant, near the city limits on the Illinois Central Railroad. The work proceeded energetically, days, nights, and Sundays, and early in April, 1897, we produced our first mash. Since then the capacity of the plant has been enlarged twice. It has run almost without interruption ever since its completion, and has proved a source of great profit to us.

After our trouble with the government was happily ended, we commenced to reconstruct the store which we had acquired by purchase over two years before. This building, with an exterior of red sandstone, stands today, on the north side of Main Street, near Second, and is an ornament to that neighborhood. Soon after we were in the building we discovered, to our surprise, that it no longer met our requirements. Our trade was growing with rapid strides. In 1888 the volume of our business amounted to about $350,000 per annum. By the time we had moved into our new quarters it had more than quadrupled. We failed in the attempt to secure more room by the purchase of the stores on either side of us. Neither did we succeed in the acquisition of a commodious warehouse on Washington Street, in the rear of our premises, which had remained tenantless for some time. The owners discovered that we needed the room badly, and took advantage of our necessity to ask exorbitant prices. Our need for additional room became more pressing from month to month—in fact, it reduced itself to a question of less business or larger quarters.

There was at that time but one vacant building on Main Street which promised to meet our requirements. It was situated near the Louisville Hotel, and was formerly owned by Bamberger, Bloom & Co. This great dry goods firm, for years a Southern business bulwark, failed soon after the panic of 1893 and went out of existence. Their building was a massive brick and stone structure, six stories high with a basement. It had been built but four years before by the old firm, in a most substantial way, with a frontage of nearly fifty feet on Main Street, running to an ell which faced on Seventh Street. It is the largest single business house on Main Street, and by reason of its enormous size was an elephant on the hands of the Mutual Life Insurance Company of New York, who had advanced one hundred thousand dollars when the building was erected and who held the mortgage.

On one Friday morning we offered seventy-five thousand dollars cash for the property and in the afternoon of the same day our offer was accepted. Mr. Jillius Bamberger told me after the purchase that the building and ground had cost Bamberger, Bloom & Co. one hundred and eighty-five thousand dollars. We promptly proceeded to reconstruct the interior so as to make it answer our purpose. We sold our old store to W. L. Weller & Sons.

At this writing we are still doing business at this same stand. It has proved an ideal home, and is conceded by people who have had occasion to visit similar places in other cities to be one of the handsomest stores in our line in the United States. We left our old place because we suffered from a decided lack of room; we moved into the new one with misgivings that we had too much. I had predicted from year to year that our firm had attained its fullest growth, and saw no avenue by which it could possibly be enlarged. Yet I have had the satisfaction of noting a comfortable increase in volume each year until November, 1907, when a panic struck this country like a whirlwind. A natural shrinkage accompanied the widespread depression that followed, and we had our share of it.

Close on the heels of panic came the Prohibition wave which inundated various States and which left a costly scar on our business. This anti-liquor craze is but another manifestation of American hysteria, and must run its course. Signs are not lacking to indicate that it will subside in due time.

Candor compels me to admit that the liquor traffic as carried on at present by the retail dealer is responsible for much of the existing prejudice. The low dive, catering to the wants of the vicious and depraved classes, should be suppressed. The American "treating habit," which is the source of so much intemperance, must be eradicated. The business of retailing liquor should be confined to localities affording efficient police protection. When these reforms shall have been put into effect, and the business shall have been placed in the hands of responsible, law-abiding, and temperate people, we may safely look forward to a period when the manufacture and sale of liquors will again become a legitimate and respected occupation. Temperance by legal enactment has made and always will make more liars than teetotalers.

As a citizen and as a lover of his fellow man, I cannot but express the hope that the man who uses intoxicants to excess will someday be treated as a social outcast. If he persists in their abuse he should be regarded in the eyes of the law as a criminal, and be segregated as the insane are. If I had to choose my occupation over again I should prefer to engage in some other line of trade, but we are all creatures of circumstance and therefore less accountable for our acts than we realize. However, in a large sense, the liquor business is as honorable to my mind as any other. The man who sells whisky is no more responsible for its abuse than the hardware dealer who sells pistols and knives, the man who sells poisons, or the farmer who raises tobacco is responsible for the effects of these things when abused.

God Almighty bestowed certain presents upon his children. If rightly and temperately used they can prove a source of benefit and pleasure; if abused they are a curse upon the head of the abuser. Therefore it is only the weak and ill-balanced persons who become the slaves of injurious habits, and for the protection of such I favor a restriction of the liquor traffic, but not its complete destruction.

I am glad to say that the Jewish race has never been deluded by the prohibition fallacy. Wine is an important factor in its ceremonials, and receives much mention in the Holy Book. It is one of the most striking characteristics of the Jew that he is temperate in his habits, and especially in the use of intoxicants. However, I have digressed again, and am in imminent danger of losing the thread of my story in the discussion of the temperance question. I will therefore return once more to my subject and record the closing chapters of my story.

NEW BLOOD
IN THE BUSINESS

While our business was growing, my brother and I were reaching the stage of life where we looked for a gradual reduction of our laborious duties. We began to cast about for younger shoulders on which to place some of our increasing responsibilities. We realized that the infusion of younger blood into a commercial enterprise is as much a necessity as is the fertilization of the soil. We were happy in the choice of our co-workers.

First came Barney Dreyfuss, who was our first cousin. He emigrated to Paducah direct from his home in Freiburg in Baden during 1883. He was then about nineteen years old. He had served his apprenticeship of three years in a German banking house, and proved to be an exceedingly apt, though at times a somewhat careless young fellow. He entered our office as assistant bookkeeper, and on our removal to Louisville became successively head bookkeeper and credit man. He showed the keenest aptitude, and rapidly developed into an exceedingly valuable and trustworthy man. In recognition of his work we allowed him a working interest in our firm in 1890, which he retained up to 1899, when, upon the urgent advice of physicians, he voluntarily relinquished his position and disposed of his interest in the firm to take up an occupation less confining. He became the principal owner and President of the Pittsburgh Baseball Club. I am proud to say he made a decided success of his enterprise. Mr. Dreyfuss resides in Pittsburgh, Penn., is very happily married and the father of an interesting family.

Others who joined forces with us were the Flarsheim brothers. They are natives of Newark, N. J., who had moved to St. Paul, Minn., and engaged in the wholesale liquor business there. Causes which it would take too long to recite here, but which could not be traced either to carelessness or want of attention to business, brought about their failure. Mr. Alfred B. Flarsheim, shortly after the collapse of his firm, applied to us for a position as representative in Minnesota. He proved to be a successful drummer and remained with us in that capacity until 1896, when we decided to open an office in New York. Being a native of the East and experienced on the road we thought him best equipped to become its manager. He remained in New York until Barney Dreyfuss was forced to relinquish his place in our office owing to ill health, when we called him to Louisville as his successor. He has been an excellent man for the place.

His elder brother, Mr. Morris H. Flarsheim, entered our employ as correspondent in the spring of 1892. He quickly acquired the necessary routine and developed by degrees into a resourceful, reliable, and tireless worker. When I say this I do not mean to disparage the good qualities of other excellent men connected with us in different capacities.

In recognition of the faithful services of these two brothers we voluntarily agreed to make them participants to a reasonable degree in the profits of the firm from 1898 on. They are still occupying the same responsible positions: Mr. Alfred B. Flarsheim as head of the credit department, and Mr. Morris H. Flarsheim as head correspondent and chief of office. I cannot close this chapter without expressing my deep gratitude for their devotion and voicing the hope that their usefulness may extend for many years undiminished.

MY SONS

I now approach a more personal phase of this narrative. Leon Solomon Bernheim, born October 10, 1875, being my oldest son, was, by reason of this fact, early selected as my successor. I had never subscribed to the belief that a college education is necessary to a good business training, but have always maintained that a good constitution, love of work, the knowledge of the value of money, the gathering of practical experience in the handling of men and merchandise, are the prime requisites in the making of a good business man. Acting on this theory, I gave Lee the opportunity of securing a good common-school education, and when he had completed his fifteenth year employed him as office boy. He applied himself to his work and made satisfactory progress, but I noticed to my surprise and to my chagrin as well, that he displayed an amount of independence in thought and action which at times produced unpleasant scenes between us.

My ideas of training are along military lines. I am an advocate of regular and early business hours, and a firm believer in methodical and systematic ways of doing things. Frankness compels me to admit that in the enforcement of these business rules I am as autocratic as the Czar of Russia. In the language of my old friend, William Rosenberg, "when I had voted, the election was over." Lee was strong-headed; he had gotten that honestly from his father. He was sensitive, which was a trait peculiar to his good mother. He had no regard for punctuality, and was generally unsystematic in his methods. To his credit be it said that his mentality was good, his habits exceptional, and his morals of a very high order. I have made it a rule to give my sons considerable latitude. I did not watch over them with the tender care so many parents lavish, and which so often softens a boy's character and deprives him of self-reliance.

Lee received the same treatment as any other office boy. He enjoyed no special privileges, and was subject to the same rigid discipline that applied to all other employees. When his

OUR LOUISVILLE RESIDENCE ON
THIRD STREET BETWEEN KENTUCKY AND ST. CATHERINE

mistakes or shortcomings were reported to me, I was at times more severe in my rebuke than with others not so close to me. It is in this respect I fear I committed a grave blunder, for my occasional harsh words of criticism cut deeply into his sensitive nature, and very likely bred a dissatisfaction which unfortunately I did not perceive and consequently failed to correct.

However, the boy made satisfactory progress. I often watched his work silently, but again I committed the grave mistake of not patting him on the back and encouraging him by a few friendly words to even better effort. I learned later in life that a few encouraging words spoken at the proper time have a wonderfully good effect on the young, and produce excellent results even in the most listless. But I believed in iron discipline, which I applied as rigorously to myself as to those who worked for me. With all my faults and shortcomings in that direction, I can truthfully say that I have never intentionally asked anything of the humblest of my employees which I was not willing to do myself.

One evening, at the expiration of his third business year, Lee, who by that time had passed his eighteenth year, asked me for a private interview. At this meeting he informed me that he had decided to give up his position. Upon my inquiry as to what he proposed to do in the future, he stated that he had decided to become an actor. I laughed, for the idea appeared absurd. I therefore treated it as a joke. It was not long, however, before I discovered, to my utter amazement, that the boy had apparently determined to turn his back on the path intended for him, and had decided to try for a career which I would, under no circumstances, sanction.

We reasoned together for hours during that unforgettable evening, but no argument, appeal, or threat that I could bring to bear seemed to make the slightest impression on him. For the first time in my life I was made aware that the authority which no one had ever questioned in my family before was slipping away from me. This incident was direful to me. Still I did not abandon hope. On the contrary, I renewed my efforts in every conceivable way to bring about a change of mind. When I discovered at last that my logic was not convincing and that my influence to a large degree had been destroyed, I brought the influence of others into requisition. His mother spent many evenings pleading with him and shedding tears of regret over his course. My brother, to whom he was greatly attached, exhausted all of his resources without the slightest success. I told my sainted friend, Rabbi Moses, of the impending danger to my son's career. He too cooperated with me in an endeavor to wean Lee away from his delusion, but without result.

I saw the futility of further effort. We therefore mutually agreed not to mention the subject for six months, and if after that period he should still be determined to fit himself for the stage I would interpose no further objection. When that period had elapsed he informed me that his mind was unchanged. I thereupon promised to furnish him the necessary means, in monthly installments, with which to equip himself to become an actor.

It was a bitter pill, but after deep reflection I concluded that if my children should decide to adopt different courses from what my judgment had laid out for them, I would in future acquiesce as good-naturedly as possible. If my decisions for them proved faulty, the responsibility for the failure would be on my shoulders, while if they followed their own ambitions they could blame no one but themselves. I have religiously followed this rule in my family, although it has caused me many heartaches.

Lee resigned his position in the fall of 1893 to enter a dramatic school in New York. He graduated three years thereafter, equipped for the stage. I have convinced myself that during those years of study he combined close application with undiminished ardor. After a wait of a few months he secured an engagement with a company which toured the smaller towns in the Northwest with more or less financial success. The company closed its season in Louisville, and it was there that I had occasion to see my son for the first and last time in the role of a professional actor. He showed some talent, and might in the course of time have developed into an artist of decided merit. But the start was not encouraging nor was the future very bright. He had discovered that in an overcrowded profession the road to the top is a long, tedious, and very trying one. He returned to New York after the company had disbanded, but failed after much search to find suitable employment.

It was then that the scales fell from his eyes. He wrote to me in a manly way, frankly acknowledging his mistake and asking for employment. It was an unexpected and joyful revelation. The mail was too slow for me to reply. I used the telegraph to congratulate him, expressing my delight to have him with me again. I arranged to place him in charge of our New York office as assistant manager and general all-around man. He came back to us the same sober, moral fellow he was before he left his home.

In the course of a few months opportunity arose by which his services could be more advantageously utilized in the home office. He returned to Louisville and worked faithfully, advancing rapidly until he reached his twenty-fifth year, when we decided to make things more attractive to him by admitting him to the firm as a partner, with a respectable interest.

Differences of opinion, however, rose between us, which at times made our intercourse rather unpleasant. I made allowances, hoping that time would soften our relations, but my hopes were not realized. On the contrary, Lee showed a defiant spirit, which at times violated every filial duty. Candor and my desire to be fair again force me to admit that I was not entirely blameless in the matter. I remained the same old high-tempered, militant autocrat. Everyone connected with our firm, not excepting my good brother, understood my weakness in this respect and treated it charitably. My own son, whose heart beat warmly for his family, would not, for reasons which I could never make clear, bring himself to the point of doing likewise. It is not my object to air grievances in these pages against any member of my family. We all have our faults and shortcomings. Children cannot expect to have ideal parents any more than parents can expect to have blameless children.

My relations with my son became strained to the breaking point. Again and again I sought to preserve the *entente cordiale*, if for no other purpose than to still the wagging tongues of the outside world. Finally I gave it up as a hopeless task. We met one Sunday morning, and it was mutually agreed that in the best interests of peace and happiness for both of us our partnership had better be dissolved. Lee therefore withdrew from our firm in 1905, and my brother and I became purchasers of his interest. He received a comfortable fortune and left for New York.

I have written somewhat in detail of this unpleasant and regrettable incident, but it is a necessary part of a narrative that aims to be a complete history of my family. In such a story it is inevitable that distasteful episodes should be chronicled. I have nothing to conceal, and there are no skeletons hidden in the closets of the Bernheims. In reciting my experiences with Lee I have sought to be fair and frank, and I have not spared myself. But the lesson and the moral of it have sunk very deeply into my mind.

Since I have written of one son, let me now go on to the story of the rest of the boys. My second son, Morris Uri Bernheim, was born on July 16, 1877. He was given an excellent education, as it was expected that he would take up a profession. When he was in his nineteenth year he entered Yale, and made very satisfactory progress in his studies. When Lee decided to prepare for a stage career, Morris, who by that time had spent two years in college, voluntarily asked to be allowed to take his place in business. Of course I readily assented.

It was interesting to me to note the difference between the two boys as they appeared at work. Both were moral, high-minded, and temperate, but Morris was much more methodical in his work, and seemed to respond more quickly to discipline from the first.

Profiting by my unhappy experience with Lee, I decided to place Morris in charge of important work that took him outside the office. Since I remained indoors at my desk, his duties brought him directly in contact with me for only a short time each day, and I figured that the chances for friction between us were slight. To a degree I was correct in this surmise, for our business intercourse continued pleasant and Morris seemed to develop admirably. He seemed to love work, had excellent control of the people under him, and everything indicated that he was qualifying for a much-needed place in our organization. In 1900 he was given a partnership corresponding with that formerly owned by his brother Lee.

But Morris had a defect in his temperament which subjected him from youth to spells of moroseness. Barring these occasional moods, we continued with what were on the whole pleasant relations. During December, 1901, he married Miss Delia Fechheimer, of Cincinnati, a very estimable young woman of excellent family. From the time of his marriage the discord between us seemed to gain fresh impetus. Slight differences became serious breaches, until one day my son asked me to step into our private office, where he informed me that he did not like the treatment he was receiving at my hands. At the same time he declared that he did not like the business he was engaged in, and had decided to withdraw from our firm. This was in June, 1903. Bernard and I became the purchasers of his share in the firm, which we had relinquished twelve years before in order to encourage the boys.

I have felt that my "militarism" was the chief cause of the dissatisfaction that led Morris to withdraw. Yet when I look back over my own career, I find that this very quality of stern stick-to-itiveness was early embedded in my makeup. It became a sort of fetish with me never to permit pleasure to interfere with my work. Seeking to mold a sensitive boy along these somewhat rigorous and uncompromising lines was perhaps an error. I might possibly have borne in mind that the circumstances of our upbringing were not the same. I was reared amid almost stern necessity, which was the mother of much character, while he was raised in an environment of complete comfort, which bordered on luxury.

My youngest son, Elbridge Palmer Bernheim, was born August 9, 1881, and was graduated from Johns Hopkins University in 1902. Immediately after his graduation he entered our employ. Like his brothers, he showed great aptitude, good morals, a fine constitution, and a commendable sense of economy. His whole smiling personality is the kind that triumphs over all obstacles. Unless I am much mistaken in my estimate of him, he will be a conspicuous success in business. When Morris retired from our business, Palmer succeeded to the vacancy in the firm caused thereby. Our relations, both in and out of business, have been very satisfactory, and I hope they may continue so without interruption. It would be indeed a calamity to me if he, emulating the example of his elder brothers, should decide to enter a new field. He married Miss Florence Marcus in April, 1906. The union has been blessed with one child, born in May, 1907.

My third son, Bertram Moses Bernheim, born February 15, 1879, was graduated from Johns Hopkins University as a Doctor of Medicine. He has the usual amount of Bernheim tenacity, is clear-headed, and I am confident will be heard from in his chosen profession. He has never tried his hand at business, and if I can help it he never will. He resides in Baltimore, where he happily married Miss Hilda Marcus. They are the parents of two children, one of whom bears my name.

THE BERNHEIM DISTILLING COMPANY

The injection of all this new blood into our business was like adding fresh fuel to a furnace. Our trade fairly leaped forward. In 1902 the annual volume of it had grown to millions, and the capital invested amounted to several millions of dollars. I have always believed that a corporation has a great advantage over a simple partnership, particularly where a large capitalization is involved. The life of a corporation is not necessarily affected by the death of a shareholder, whereas in a partnership the sudden demise of a partner may seriously threaten or even jeopardize the business.

My brother and I had the better part of our lives behind us; we were the principal owners of the capital in the business, and realizing the many disadvantages of a partnership, we decided, in 1903, to establish a corporation, under the name of the Bernheim Distilling Company. The paid-up capital was two millions of dollars. At the first election I was chosen President and Bernard was made Vice-president.

I have always been deeply mindful of the loyalty and service of our employees, and with the establishment of the corporation we decided to admit many of our old coworkers as stockholders. We agreed to carry the stock until they were ready to pay for it with their savings. It is a matter of great pleasure for me to be able to record that in this way, a number of deserving men have been able to share in our profits.

As the affairs of the new corporation expanded we found it to our advantage to acquire new properties. We became interested in the formation of the Commercial Distilling Company of Terre Haute, Indiana, so as to obtain spirits at manufacturers' cost, and in 1906 we purchased the Warwick Distillery at Silver Creek, in Madison County. We also bought a smaller interest in the rye distillery of the Baltimore Distilling Company, located in Baltimore.

As I write this history, the Bernheim Distilling Company is more than maintaining its reputation for increasing activity and growing prosperity. Its earning capacity is large and steady and its financial status unshakable. I have every reason to believe that with its present organization it will not only hold but increase its commanding commercial position.

At this point in my narrative I am aware of the fact that in my desire to present a completely connected account of my own life I have had to digress to somewhat prosaic business details, but they are so thoroughly bound up with my own affairs that to ignore them would be to leave a large void in my experiences.

Happily I can hereafter forego all talk of trade, and become as it were the historian of days that, through sentiment and tender association, were among the happiest of my life. Although chronologically I shall have to retrace my steps, I feel that the reader will perhaps bear with me as I turn back the pages of memory to the time when life and love were both young—

"To dream the dreams of youth again,

When we were twenty-one."

PART I

THE ROMANCE OF MY YOUTH

It will be recalled that when I began my business career at Paducah I had just passed my twenty-third year, and social life had many charms for me very naturally. But in those days society did not make such exacting demands as it does today. In a town the size of Paducah simplicity marked all gayeties. Such luxuries as fine clothes, carriages for parties, and elaborate gifts were almost unheard of. And yet beneath unpretentious exteriors loyal hearts leaped to happy responses.

The wardrobes of the young women were typical of the simplicity of the times. If a girl had a few fresh calico dresses to wear during the week and a nice all-wool merino dress for Sunday wear her outfit was deemed almost complete. Hats were bought only twice a year, and they ranged in price from two to five dollars apiece. Elaborate creations of the milliner's art, costing twenty-five or fifty dollars, would have created a sensation and would have been regarded as the very height of extravagance.

There were many diversions to bring the young people together. Between the ordinary parties, where everybody met for a general good time, there were balls. Yet even for an important event like this no very special preparations were required. The young girls appeared in their best frocks and the young men in their Sunday clothes. In summer there were many outdoor picnics. We enjoyed the luxury of a theatrical performance only at long intervals, and then in an ill-equipped, unattractive hall. But life sped quickly and joyously for me those first years at Paducah.

It was in 1870 that the town received the welcome influx of a group of charming Jewish families, which gave a better tone to our social life. Among the additions to our circle were the families of Alexander and Isaac Levi, who came from St.

Louis; my uncles Benjamin Weille and M. Livingston, who had brought their families back from New York; Mr. Morris Uri, who had moved from Cincinnati, and several others whose names I do not remember.

Of the newcomers the Uris seemed from the start to be the most attractive, and they were destined to play a very important part in my young life, which was then shaping. The family consisted of the parents, one son, and five daughters. The ages of the children ranged from five to eighteen years. The name Uri was not unfamiliar to me. I had often heard it mentioned by my good aunt Jeannette Weille, for it was at the Uri home in Louisville that she met Mr. Weille, whom she afterward married. Mrs. Uri was a brunette of medium build, attractive in features, with a cheerful disposition and most engaging manners. She radiated kindliness. One quickly recognized in her the ideal mother, idolized by husband and children alike.

The family was not in particularly affluent circumstances, for Mr. Uri had been a sort of plaything of fortune. He was born in 1819, had enjoyed a good education, and had many delightful personal qualities. In many respects he reminded me of the portraits of Abraham Lincoln, for he was tall, almost lank, and wore a beard which made his resemblance to the great War President all the more striking. His experiences are worth recounting. Like many other ambitious young Europeans, he left his home in Hechingen, Hohenzollern, Germany, in 1848, and came to America.

After serving an apprenticeship as peddler in New York State he set out for the West, but gravitated South and settled in Paducah. Here, in partnership with his brother Abraham, who had followed him to the States, he opened a small country store. Their business prospered, and they were enabled to move to Louisville and embark in the wholesale dry goods business with Mr. Israel Heyman, the firm becoming Heyman & Uri. Their store was located on Main Street, near Fifth. The change promised well. Under the direction of Mr. Uri satisfactory progress was made until the Civil War broke out. Then all trade in the South stood still, and the young concern was wiped out of existence.

After the failure Mr. Uri returned to Paducah, reopened his old business, and soon after became a partner of Wolf Brothers, who had built up a considerable business in the region south of Paducah and bordering on the Cumberland and Tennessee rivers.

Once more the Nemesis of war pursued Mr. Uri, for General Nathan Bedford Forrest visited Paducah during his raid in Western Kentucky and carried off much of the stock of the stores there. More than this, his advent created such a feeling of insecurity that many merchants wound up their affairs and removed to a region more immune from sudden and costly invasion. The firm of Wolf Brothers was dissolved. Again Mr. Uri moved to Louisville, this time to engage with some partners in the wholesale boot and shoe business. He had sufficient capital remaining to discharge his share of the debts of the defunct firm of Heyman & Uri, which was an act eminently characteristic of his high business integrity.

With the close of the Civil War came apprehension and disaster to commerce. The currency situation was in a confused tangle and there was endless fluctuation in gold. As business order came out of all this chaos of reconstruction, many firms who had been weakened by bad debts in the South and by the shrinkage of prices of stocks were forced to the wall. Mr. Uri's firm tried manfully to stem the adverse tide, and for a time held its own somewhat precariously, first in Louisville and then in Cincinnati. But the odds were too great, and it was forced into receivership.

It was at this unhappy time that Mr. Uri bethought himself of the pleasant little Kentucky town on the banks of the Ohio River which had on two previous occasions offered him a haven for his wife and children. Thither he again turned his steps, and with the assistance of his good friend, the late Nathan Bloom, of Bamberger, Bloom & Co., he started a dry goods store on a modest scale. There was now every reason why Mr. Uri, despite his many buffets from evil fortune, should have looked forward confidently to the future, when in less than a year after his new start he was dealt a tragic blow. On July 22, 1871, his wife died, after a short illness. She was only in her forty-third year. Through the years of his changing fortunes she had been his helpmeet, steadfast in every sense, and her loss at the time when he most needed encouragement was a crushing blow. It is told among her children that on the day of her untimely death, and in the presence of their oldest daughter, he leaned tenderly over the dying form, whispering so that it was heard all over the room, "Malche, ich homme dir nach." (Amelia, I will follow you soon.)

A year had scarcely elapsed before he made good this promise and followed her to the Great Beyond. The responsibility of the family so tragically bereft of both parents fell upon the shoulders of the eldest child, Mr. Nathan M. Uri, who was then about twenty-one years of age. Manfully he assumed the charge and became the head of the orphaned household. The eldest daughter, who was in her eighteenth year, resolutely took up the burdens of her four younger sisters, and carried on the domestic affairs with such tact, judgment, and good sense as to become an object of the deepest interest to me.

My undisguised admiration for this self-possessed, independent, unselfish American girl who had proved her mettle in this trying ordeal ripened into love. After a courtship which extended over several months I was made happy by the thrilling knowledge that my love was returned. In November, 1872, we secretly plighted our troth. I was twenty-four, she eighteen.

With her advent into my life, the whole world took on a new glamor for me. I was not richly endowed with worldly goods, but I had hope, faith, and the inspiring knowledge that I had chosen a mate worthy of my highest ambition. Our wedding, which took place September 23, 1874, was one of the social events of Paducah. *The Daily Kentuckian* devoted two columns to a vivid description of it. I carefully preserved a copy of the article for years, but unfortunately it has since been lost. Paducah's first Rabbi, Doctor Leopold, performed the ceremony in the then newly finished synagogue, built by the first Jewish Congregation of the community.

In fact, our wedding was the first to take place in a Jewish place of worship in that city. The ceremony was not lacking in any detail to make it complete. The music was furnished by the Temple choir, of which the bride was an active member. After the wedding service had been performed the company proceeded to the Concordia club-house, where a supper had been prepared by Mrs. Charles Unrath, who enjoyed quite a local reputation as a cook and caterer.

My limited means did not permit of the extravagance of a wedding tour, so we went at once to the modest frame cottage of five rooms, which was owned by Mr. Henry Weil, whose tenants we were for nine years. Then I was able to provide a home of my own. There have been some big and swelling events in my life in later years, when I heard the plaudits of many men, but there is not one that I recall with more exquisite pleasure than that moment when first I led the wife of my heart to the sanctuary that we could call our home.

"*Heimath und Liebe*"—the twin stars that guide every true romance—had at last shown me the way to happiness.

MY MOTHER

In addition to setting up a shining milestone in my life's journey, my marriage marked the first public appearance of my mother in this country. With characteristic devotion and self-sacrifice she had sold all her personal and real estate in Freiburg, cut loose from the treasured associations of her native land, and made the long, hard journey to Kentucky, willing and glad—in her desire to afford me pleasure—to exchange the long-established use and well-seasoned comforts of her old home for the more primitive accommodations of a somewhat small and raw American town. Her action in this instance was one of an almost innumerable list of similar acts of affectionate service which betokened her great heart and boundless goodness. She reached Paducah ten days before my wedding, bringing with her the two children of her second marriage; Herman, who was then a boy of fourteen and who quickly learned to make himself useful in our store, and Sara, who was twelve and still in school.

After a rest of a few days at the residence of her sister, Mrs. Benjamin Weille, my mother established herself in a comfortable cottage, and the transplanted little family took root in the new and friendly Kentucky soil. Bernard acted as head of the household, and right glad was he to be able to sit down again at a table where the fragrant and appetizing delicacies of boyhood days were once more served to him by loving hands. Those were happy days for all the Bernheims. With growing success our family affection had only bloomed more richly.

My mother's home became the rallying place for the whole clan. No celebration was real or complete unless it was held there. The joyous anniversaries of birth; the glad greetings to the New Year; the ceremonial observances of religious festivals—all transpired under her hospitable and generous roof, and remain today as cherished recollections.

Mother had a rare faculty of attracting young and old alike, for she had the natural charm of real graciousness. Her appreciation and love for my wife were instantaneous; from the moment they met, their relations were intimate and devoted. Our little ones adored her. To them "Grosmutter" was a sort of patron saint, and they flocked to her kindly arms as soon as they knew how to walk.

In 1884 she returned to Germany to visit her brothers and to look once more upon dear and familiar scenes. On her return she frankly admitted that she was glad, as she expressed it, to be "home again," and nothing could have induced her to reside permanently in Europe again. So adaptable was she that within a few years she had become an enthusiastic American.

She had the happiness of witnessing the marriage of all her children. To me was given the great privilege of having her as an honored guest under my roof during the last years of her beautiful life. It was there, surrounded by all her loved ones, that she breathed her last, on May 25, 1889, in her sixty-second year. In her death, sorrow laid its heavy hand on my immediate family for the first time in almost a generation. We had been peculiarly immune from sad visitations, and were correspondingly thankful.

With my mother's passing there slipped out of life a brave and gentle soul, whom to know was to love, revere, and honor.

MY WIFE

Just as circumstances gave me the saintliest of mothers, so did destiny lead me to the most ideal of wives. Rarely is it the good fortune of man to be so favored in the choice of his help-meet. From that day, nearly forty years ago, when first she came into my life, the world has been a better and dearer place. Her courage, faith, sacrifice, and endeavor have made possible whatever success I have achieved. Her early household economies contributed as much to my material prosperity as the profits we derived from a young and struggling business by hard work.

Wise in counsel, generous in forgiveness, she was diplomat, peacemaker, and general conserver of our home. Where I was the autocrat, she was the gentle, brooding dove. It was due to her effective ministrations that I was enabled to devote an undivided attention to business.

As our children came, her loveliness only ripened. Maternity invested her with a rich and beautiful dignity. Her loyalty as wife was only equaled by her devotion as mother. I have already enumerated our four sons. Three daughters have also blessed our union. They are Amelia, born November 23, 1884, Helen, born April 4, 1886, and Marguerite, born November 26, 1888. At this writing only two of our seven children remain unmarried—Lee, the eldest, and Marguerite, the youngest; Millie having become the wife of Julian S. Rauh, of Cincinnati. Their union has been blessed with one daughter, Helen, born December 9, 1906. My daughter Helen married Albert S. Roth, of Cincinnati, on June 3, 1908. Both of my daughters have chosen sturdy, self-reliant, and good men, and their futures promise well.

We are the happy grandparents of five girls and one boy, the last mentioned having arrived January 7, 1909, at the home of Doctor Bert Bernheim in Baltimore. He bears my name, and I hope he will carry it worthily.

It is not often that a man is able to look back over such a married life as has been my lot. Yet when I look at the dear comrade of all these precious years I need not wonder at my supreme happiness. Though the frosts of many winters have whitened her hair, her face is still free from wrinkles, her skin is clear, her fine blue eyes as bright as on that day, long ago, when I first looked into them and saw therein the light of my future. Passing time has only illumined her loveliness.

My wife has truly beaconed my path with love and service and lightened my burdens with faith and cheer. Were I to coin my gratitude into words, this chapter would be an unending serial.

MY POLITICS AND RELIGION

HOMEWOOD, ANCHORAGE, KENTUCKY, 1908

For lack of more human material this chronicle now nears its end. Before I close I shall presume a little more upon the forbearance of my descendants by reverting once more to my own affairs. I do so only in the hope that some germ of my business, political, or domestic creeds may develop useful activities in coming Bernheim generations.

I believe that every American should be honestly interested in politics, for a strong, sane, healthy political activity is ever the safeguard of a democracy. At the time of my arrival in this country in 1867 I affiliated myself with the Republican Party, because it stood for liberty in that it had freed the negro of his shackles. Being of a race that had long known the oppressor, this one principle alone appealed to me with great force. I have never severed my connection with the Republican Party; yet I have always respected any man's beliefs, if only they were sincere and honest.

The opportunities to enjoy various political and public honors have come to me frequently, but I have almost invariably declined them. Up to my fortieth year my business kept me away from home the greater part of the year, and shortly thereafter my health suffered so seriously from overwork that I had to forego any outside demands on my strength and energy.

I have made it an ironclad rule not to accept any position of trust unless I was prepared to give it all the time and attention that its importance demanded. My friend, Governor W. O. Bradley, the first Republican Governor in the history of Kentucky, prevailed upon me to accept the post of Commissioner of the State Asylum for the Insane at Lakeland, and I served in that capacity for four years. The office was purely one of honor, but it had high responsibilities and duties, which I felt it incumbent upon me as a citizen of Kentucky not to shirk. It was a pleasure to render this service. Although I have been more or less active in my party for many years, this is the only political office I have ever held. I have, however, been a contributor to all the campaign funds, and have participated in many conventions, acting always on the theory that to be a loyal citizen a man must be interested in the fundamental institutions of his country. In such interest and cooperation lies the real hope of pure and efficient government by and for the people.

My intense pride in and loyalty to the faith of my fathers found expression soon after I became well established in America. I began to read and later became an occasional contributor to the *American Israelite*, which was published in Cincinnati. This admirable periodical was edited by Rabbi Isaac M. Wise, the "Old Man Eloquent" of our race in the New World.

His was a noble and patriarchal figure; I had the honor to know him. It was Doctor Wise who led the great movement for Jewish Reform. He had the foresight to know that the old-fashioned Oriental form of Jewish worship was out of place in our progressive, Occidental civilization, and; that to hold the interest and claim the loyalty of the rising generation in Israel it had to be adapted to the advanced and enlightened spirit of the age. To do this meant no compromise with cherished traditions or time-honored teachings. His wisdom prevailed, and today wherever advanced Hebrews meet for worship the name of Rabbi Wise is blessed.

I agreed heartily with his views. When the first Jewish Congregation was formed in Paducah in 1870 I had an active share in its organization. I served first as Secretary and later as President. I shaped its course toward the Reformed ranks. When I moved to Louisville in 1888 I immediately joined the Congregation Adath Israel, and I have the distinction of having been one of its officers.

But no honor that my connection with this synagogue has brought me compares with the privilege of having had a long and close association with its beloved pastor, the late lamented Rabbi Adolph Moses. I count myself fortunate in having been included among his friends. We shall not soon look upon the like of this great and good man again. He was more than a minister, he was an eloquent and impassioned leader of the hosts of men. His scholarship was ripe; his humanity was broad and illuminating; his tolerance was generous; and his whole life a rich outpouring of high and loyal service for his race. Jew and Gentile alike delighted to revere and respect him. People of all creeds came to listen to the words of wisdom that fell from his devoted lips. I am indebted to him for many hours of inspiration and instruction, and our friendly relations continued with increasing intimacy until his untimely death on January 7, 1902.

Through my influence, and with his hearty cooperation, the movement for Sunday services at the Temple was carried through. When the subject was first broached the conservatives looked at it askance. They feared it was too radical. However, Doctor Moses, who yielded to none in his fidelity to Jewish traditions, was broad-minded enough to realize that in these services lay the real hope of attracting the younger generation of Judaism to the standard of their Faith.

It was impossible for the ancient habits of the orthodox Jew to compete with the customs of the country in which he lived. No custom was more fixed than that which made Sunday a general day of relaxation. It was a question of getting the Israelite to church on that day or not at all. We believed that it would stimulate interest in our whole creed, and would be attractive alike to men and to women.

After a campaign of education extending over some years we carried our point. The innovation was successful from the start, and has proved in every sense a wise and helpful step in the constructive as well as spiritual uplift of our race. It is only due to Rabbi Moses to say that much of its favor grew out of his own large share in making the Sunday services richly interesting and fruitful. His sermons were pieces of almost inspired literature, and the memory of their eloquence and learning will linger long among those who were fortunate enough to hear them.

The Sunday service for the Hebrew is part of what I think must be a larger plan for the future working out of the vast relation between people of different faiths the world over. It symbolizes the spirit of liberality, generosity, and reform. Without these attributes creeds will never unbend, and for that reason cannot become closely related. The most thrilling prospect before us today is the vision of the Brotherhood of Man, and it is by toleration alone that this vast and kindling harmony of races and creeds can be achieved. In this respect America and Australia lead, and they will be the pioneers for the rest of the world.

MY BROTHER

It is peculiarly fitting, perhaps, that I should conclude this chronicle of long and loving association with some tribute to him who has been my comrade through most of the years of my life. I refer to my brother Bernard, the playmate of my youth, the balance-wheel of my more strenuous days, and always my discreet and sympathetic coworker.

He was born in Schmieheim on December 13, 1850, and there is a difference of only two years in our ages. In our boyhood we were almost inseparable. Early in life the distinct differences in our characteristics manifested themselves. He was large-hearted and amiable, while I was impetuous and dominating. It followed that there were many conflicts in those early days, that were not always waged with words. But peace always followed.

It was the intention of our family to prepare Bernard for a professional career, but a career in Germany in those days did not have the tremendous possibilities of one in our own great Republic. At best he could have become only a petty provincial official. He had the good fortune to find employment as clerk in the office of a lawyer in Freiburg, where he earned good wages at a time when money was most needed to supply the necessities of our family. He remained at this post until I summoned him to Paducah in the winter of 1870, where we jointly took up the task of making our way in the world. He was green and raw when he landed in Kentucky, and hardly knew the English alphabet. But with an aptitude and willingness which have always marked him he developed swiftly under my tutelage, and in less than ninety days I made a pretty good bookkeeper and correspondent out of him.

How we struggled together in that new land, how by frugality and thrift and industry we slowly but surely reached the point where we branched out for ourselves, and how the increasing years only expanded our fortunes, has already been told in these pages.

With the growth of our business the desire to revisit the

BERNARD BERNHEIM AT 58

scenes of his youth grew on him, and he made frequent trips to Europe. It was in one of these journeys that he found his wife, who was Miss Rosa Dreyfuss, the eldest daughter of our uncle, Mr. Samuel Dreyfuss. They have been blessed with five children, the eldest, Lynn B. Bernheim, being an officer in the United States Navy, and the second, Frank, a valued employee of the Bernheim Distilling Company.

As I look in retrospect over the long years of my association with Bernard, I see more clearly and gratefully all the large and generous qualities which have endeared him to me always. No two people could be more opposite in temperament than my brother and myself. He was always conservative, and less ambitious than I, preferring ease and comfort to the increasing responsibilities and worries of an extensive business. While

I gladly acknowledged his philosophy, I invariably opposed this idea. I believed in a vast trade empire. His conservatism, however, often kept me out of ventures which later events proved would have been unwise and unprofitable.

Quite naturally, in such a lengthy and close association, differences have arisen between us, but they were always of brief duration and swiftly subsided, largely because of his sunny nature and great heart, which never carried a grudge or bore malice. I realize that I have caused him many hours of anxiety and perhaps pain, and it is a pleasure to me now not only to set down this sincere expression of my regret for these occurrences, but to voice as well my earnest hope that he will be spared to me and his family for many years to come.

Men of the type of Bernard are rare in this bustling age of selfish commercialism. He is as gentle and forgiving as he is big and manly. All the high qualities of honor, loyalty, and integrity meet in his tender nature and make him loved and admired. Of him I can say, as the poet Byron said of his friend Sheridan, the great playwright—

"Nature made but one such man."

THE GIFT OF THE JEFFERSON MONUMENT

THE OFFER
AND THE ACCEPTANCE

IN the career of every man, even in that of the merchant devoted to the prosaic pursuits of trade, there are always a few great moments that stand out in his memory with peculiar vividness. In the preceding narrative I have spoken of some events that stirred and moved me to profound emotion or feeling. But these were purely personal experiences.

I come now to one other occasion, perhaps the most conspicuous of my life, in which my brother had full share. I refer to our gift of the Thomas Jefferson monument to the city of Louisville. This was an act conceived in gratitude and actuated by patriotic feeling. The appreciation of it, so happily and generously expressed by the citizens of the great Commonwealth which has given us sanctuary and success, made the presentation all the more memorable.

It is more in the hope that my posterity may be inspired by the motives which led to this gift, rather than by the mere spectacular features of the occasion, that I set down the whole story here. The traditions of a nation are in its memorials, and the faith of a people may be exalted by tangible reminders of its departed leaders. If coming generations of Kentuckians gather from the heroic figure of the "Sage of Monticello" the lesson of real democracy and loyal civic duty, then my brother and I are content.

The record of the Jefferson Monument can best be told perhaps in the terms of the official documents and newspaper accounts. The formal tender was made by us in the following letter to the Board of Park Commissioners:

Louisville, Ky., Sept. 18, 1899.

To the Hon. Charles P. Weaver, Mayor, and the Board of Park Commissioners of the City of Louisville—Gentlemen: Prompted by the desire to do something in honor of the city and State of our adoption, we have had in contemplation for some years a design, in the final execution of which we feel the time is now opportune to ask your cooperation.

In common with great numbers of our fellow citizens throughout the land, we are ardent admirers of the life and works of Thomas Jefferson, and believing that art, and particularly that art which exhibits to the people an ever-living likeness of a great national personage, is an important factor in their education, we have determined to offer to the city of Louisville a bronze statue in heroic size of Thomas Jefferson.

With this end in view, about three years ago we intrusted the work to the famous American sculptor, the Chevalier Moses Ezekiel, who has been knighted by the King of Italy for his achievements in art, and he has been ever since almost continuously engaged in its execution at his studio in Rome. The artist has completed his part of the task; the statue and its accompanying pedestal are now being cast in bronze by Gladenbeck, of Berlin, and we expect that the entire work will be finished within the next few months. We believe from all we can learn that the completed work will be a fine specimen of the distinguished sculptor's skill, and a faithful representation of one of the world's greatest statesmen.

It is perhaps appropriate to outline briefly some of the more notable features of the work. The statue in bronze will be nine feet in height, and will represent Jefferson in his thirty-third year, the time of his life when he wrote the Declaration of Independence, and will exhibit him holding that immortal document in his hand and about to offer it to the first Congress, assembled in Independence Hall.

The statue will stand on a pedestal in bronze, also nine feet in height, and this, in turn, will rest upon a sub-base and steps of dark, highly polished native American granite, six feet in height, thus making the whole twenty-four feet in height.

The bronze pedestal will take the form of the famous Liberty Bell, and on the sides of the bell the sculptor has modeled four female figures representing Liberty, Equality, Justice, and the Brotherhood of Man—those four great cardinal principles which were so dear to the heart of Thomas Jefferson, and which are now a part of the very life of the American people.

We propose to present this work, complete in all its details, to the city of Louisville on the Fourth of July, 1900, and in connection therewith, and also in order that the work may be suitably maintained and preserved, we will establish and place in the hands of proper trustees a permanent fund of $10,000, to be invested in United States or other safe bonds selected by the trustees. It is our desire that the income of this fund be applied to the maintenance of the statue, to the celebration at its base of each recurring Fourth of July with appropriate ceremonies, and to an award on that day of a prize or prizes to those pupils of the public schools of Louisville who shall prepare the best essay commemorative of some national event or character connected with the life and times of Thomas Jefferson; but these are matters of detail, which will be left to the trustees for their determination.

We ask of you and the city of Louisville only one thing in connection with this work, a proper site for the location of this statue. The artist, when in Louisville, himself selected as the most appropriate site the center of the plot of ground in Central Park immediately west of the lodge at the Fourth Avenue entrance to the park. We highly approve this selection, and earnestly ask of you that you will take all such measures as will enable us to obtain that location as the site of the statue. It will take some months to obtain and place in position the necessary granite base for the statue, and we therefore beg to be advised as early as may be when we may make use of the site selected. We are, gentlemen, with great respect, etc.

Isaac W. Bernheim,
Bernard Bernheim.

Their reply was as follows:

Louisville, Ky., Sept. 20, 1899.

Messrs. Isaac W. Bernheim and Bernard Bernheim, Louisville, Ky.—Dear Sirs: The Board of Park Commissioners have very great pleasure in owning receipt of your valued communication of the 18th inst., coming to us through His Honor, Mayor Weaver.

It is rare in any community, and altogether exceptional in our own, that such public spirit and personal generosity find expression. In all ages the virtues of great men have been perpetuated before the eyes of their compatriots by outward symbols expressive of their lives and the benefits by them conferred on their country. In Rome and Greece these symbols took on the pleasing shape of monuments erected by the State, so artistically designed and gracefully executed that today they form the basis of true sculptural art. So well recognized is this method of commemorating the virtues of great men, and at the same time holding them up as examples to be followed, that from the greatest cities to the smaller village are to be found some statue erected to the memory of its greatest citizen. In our own country, in most instances, the honor of commemorating the deeds of our great men is left to the generosity of citizens whose love of country is marked by gifts worthy of the subject and of the object to be attained. And it is from this source, gentlemen, that comes the magnificent offer embodied in your letter.

It is particularly gratifying that you have chosen to give patriotic direction to your munificence in commemorating the greatness of the author of the Declaration of American Independence, and in providing for an annual educational incentive to the youth of our public schools, whose love of country shall be stimulated by gathering on the great national holiday about the statue which your personal generosity contributes as commemorative of the public virtues of the man whose national achievements are an essential part of our country's history.

We note that the great sculptor has himself selected as the most beautiful and appropriate site for the erection of the statue of Jefferson, the spot indicated in Central Park. In accepting now the trust with which you honor Louisville, we are obliged to admonish you that the grounds whose great beauty has excited the enthusiasm and admiration of Chevalier Moses Ezekiel is not yet the public domain, but by agreement with the DuPont heirs the question of the value of the property has been submitted to the courts, and when this is determined the people of Louisville will through municipal direction provide means for acquiring the great public pleasure ground whose exquisite beauty has attracted the attention of the sculptor.

For more than five and twenty years, by the courtesy of the family whose head has donated the DuPont Manual Training School to the public use, the public has enjoyed their private grounds. The time has now come when the public will obtain them as their own, and your great generosity will furnish the first work of art to adorn the park.

Thanking you again in behalf of the public, we have the honor to be, dear sirs, very truly yours,

Board of Park Commissioners,
BY: John B. Castleman, President.

At the same time the Board of Park Commissioners adopted the following resolutions:

The Board of Park Commissioners of the city of Louisville, having received the communication from Messrs. Isaac W. Bernheim and Bernard Bernheim addressed to His Honor, the Mayor, and this Board jointly, in which they declare a purpose of donating to the city, to be placed in one of the parks, a statue of Thomas Jefferson, takes this method of expressing its sincere and cordial appreciation of the beautiful sentiment and generous public spirit that have moved these citizens to make the gift.

Coming from a foreign country as poor boys, they have by their industry, sagacity, and faithful adherence to correct business principles, become prominent men of affairs in the city of their adoption. Now wishing to show their goodwill in this substantial, public way, we cannot refrain from an expression of our hearty indorsement of their commendable course.

Therefore, be it resolved by this Board, That we, on behalf of the citizens of Louisville, most sincerely thank Messrs. Bernheim for their generosity, and most sincerely commend their public spirit.

That we make such provisions as may be necessary to carry into effect their every wish in connection with the gift.

That we cooperate with the city authorities in fully carrying out such wishes as may be expressed in suitably observing the occasion of the reception and dedication

of the gift. And be it further

Resolved, That an engrossed copy of these resolutions be prepared and presented to Messrs. Bernheim.

JEFFERSON MONUMENT, DEDICATED 1900

THE COMMERCIAL CLUB'S TRIBUTE

Following the announcement of our gift, my brother and I received many evidences of the appreciation of our fellow-citizens. None, however, was more grateful than the honor conferred on us by the Commercial Club at its New Year's reception held January 2, 1900. A large and brilliant company assembled at the Louisville Hotel parlors for the occasion.

Mr. William R. Belknap, the President, in his opening address made the following statement:

Years ago the Commercial Club placed the name of Isaac W. Bernheim on its list of honorary members. His liberality to all worthy causes before being asked was then recognized. We are here in recognition of the fact that the Messrs. Bernheim have presented to the city a statue of Thomas Jefferson. It will speak to us and to future generations of the greatness of American citizenship.

He then read the resolution, which had been engrossed and framed, and presented it to us. It was as follows:

The Commercial Club, representing in large numbers the financial, commercial, and manufacturing interests of the city of Louisville, desires to tender to you on behalf of all classes, congratulations and felicitations upon the munificent gift, the statue of Thomas Jefferson, recently tendered by you to this city, and to give expression to the gratitude and admiration of your fellow-townsmen for this splendid offering for the ornamentation of the city and the education of the people of Kentucky.

In this great republic, now the teacher of all the world in the best methods of government, and wherever the glorious conflicts for liberty shall be felt, the name of him who, in the Declaration of Independence, America's title-deed of liberty, wrote these immortal words: "All men are created equal, and governments derive their just powers from the consent of the governed," shall be as eternal as Time itself.

We sincerely trust that this superb gift of yours will stimulate like offerings from others of your fellow citizens and prove the forerunner of many similar donations, and thus through your influence create in Louisville the manifestation of a municipal pride and liberality which will make it both beautiful and renowned, and bring to you increased delight and pleasure.

In behalf of the 250,000 people of Louisville, in behalf of the city's highest and truest public spirit, and in behalf of its future commercial development and increase, and in behalf of all that makes nobler and better citizenship, and more devoted and loyal patriotism, we thank and congratulate you upon this splendid offering to Liberty's great apostle and to this city, which holds you in such high esteem.

> W. R. BELKNAP, President.
> W. C. VAN PELT, Secretary.

Committee.—John J. Saunders, Chairman; Enos Spencer, Logan C. Murray, W. J. Lyons, Geo. C. Norton, Chas. P. Weaver, Mayor, Clarence Dallam, Bennett H. Young.

It was a proud moment for both of us. I did my best to do justice to it in the following speech:

Mr. Chairman and Gentlemen: During the winter of '96, while abroad, you conferred upon me the distinction of electing me an honorary member of the Commercial Club. To be thus honored by an organization counting among its members all that is best, most progressive, liberal and wide awake, giving tone and character to the community, is indeed an honor of which any one might feel proud, and which I treasure today as one of the highest awards bestowed upon me as a citizen of

Louisville.

This morning my brother and myself are again honored by your organization, and for this honor my good brother and my humble self thank you most sincerely and from the bottom of our hearts.

I have asked myself whether I am really deserving of all these honors. We have done only our duty, giving back to the community a part of our modest fortunes, which God Almighty, from whom all blessings flow, has bestowed upon us.

It has been claimed, and it may be true, that Louisville can boast of but few men of a conspicuous public spirit, but this is rather the result of conditions than the fault of her citizens. The Civil War left this community in an impoverished condition, its commerce and manufactures paralyzed, its merchants reduced in resources and disheartened. "The Gateway of the South" led, unfortunately, to that section which was unmistakably poor. Desolation, waste, uncertainty, despair, and utter helplessness to cope with new conditions was the order of the day.

Louisville and the South had to begin anew, and like all new beginners, made many costly errors. Still there was a steady progress made during the few years following the close of the war. The panic of 1873 intervened, and with it came a period of depression almost unparalleled in the history of the country. Everybody suffered, but Louisville and the South suffered most, because, like a new country, its resources were comparatively slender and its credit, therefore, was most seriously affected. It was only during the last years of the '70s the cloud began to lift and the true American spirit began to assert itself.

The patriotic Pennsylvanian, Kelly, it was who first drew the attention of the country at large to the magnificent possibilities of the iron industry of the

South. We learned from Pennsylvania! A handful of Massachusetts cotton spinners encouraged us in the operation of the cotton mills. We learned from Massachusetts! And thus, by degrees, we became thoroughly saturated with the aims and tendencies of progressive Americanism. We learned to be tolerant in our political views. Republican and Democrat began to know each other better and esteem each other higher. Politics ceased to be a factor, and business began to take the lead.

In all these years Louisville and the country back of the "Gateway of the South" laid the foundation for substantial growth and solid prosperity. This foundation—it took a generation—is laid well and deep, and now, gentlemen, we are above ground; the structure is not completed—it will take another generation to make this city great in all its appointments and the peer of any inland city of this continent.

Modern Americanism produces public-spirited men of the type of Peabody, Armour, Carnegie, Rockefeller, Stanford, Sutro, and hundreds of others. Louisville will have her full share of them, because with the development of the South the opportunities for building up greater fortunes will present themselves, and greater fortunes beget greater liberality and greater public spirit.

That sturdy Americanism which these last ten years has accomplished what it took other nations generations to accomplish, will and has set up a new and higher standard of civic pride and public spirit, but while this is true, we should ever remember that what has made this a possibility is the heritage handed down to us by the founders of this glorious country and its principles of freedom.

The declaration that "all men are created equal" has acted as a magnet, to which was drawn with irresistible force from the older nations that material which is best and most valuable in the human family. Emigrants, poor in purse, but rich in brawn and muscle, possessing less of the higher education and more of practical common sense, religious but not bigoted, ambitious but not selfish, loving Liberty and Labor for Liberty and Labor's sake, have made this country their abiding place.

Here, under Liberty's banner, we are taking the former slave, providing him with an education and fitting him out as a desirable citizen. The poor lad from Ireland, the hardy Englishman and Scotchman, the phlegmatic German, the oppressed from all lands, are by the magic touch of Liberty, within a surprisingly short space of time, converted into patriotic and useful American citizens. We owe this to the founders of this country.

To perpetuate these saintly principles, to hold them fresh in the minds of our people, we have decided to erect a statue of Thomas Jefferson. The principles of the Declaration of Independence are as old as the Bible itself, but Jefferson—the humane Jefferson—gave them force and effect. This giant and prophetic intellect recognized no distinction between color or race, between creed or class. To him, therefore, struggling humanity owes a debt of gratitude which will ever fill the human breast.

Our great warriors on land and sea have been honored with monuments in many places, but to us has been left the pleasant and patriotic duty to perpetuate fittingly his memory and to couple therewith an additional incentive for the growing generations of our public schools, to keep burning brightly the light of Freedom and Liberty.

The schools are the nurseries of the Republic; as long as our children are taught to draw the lessons for the future from the experience of our glorious past, as long as they are imbued with the spirit and principles which guided their forefathers in the upbuilding of our institutions, our countrymen need not fear for its safety. This we hope to accomplish, in a limited degree at least, by the setting aside of a sufficient fund for the distribution of prizes to the pupils of our public schools for the best essay on different great national characters and events.

The monument to Thomas Jefferson is expected to foster two great virtues, namely, a love of country and a love for art. The place which we had fondly expected to secure for our donation has, to the deepest regret of many, been so far denied us. We have no reproach for any one; the question was overshadowed by more exciting issues, which had to find their adjustment at the ballot-box. We feel that we can safely trust that the final verdict of our citizens at some future day will be more favorable to the cause. Central Park must become the property of the city, with or without the monument. To allow it to be divided into building lots would be a crime from which coming generations would suffer and for which they would have just cause to reproach us.

It is the one spot within the city which has been preserved in all the glory of primitive Kentucky nature. True, we have other parks, grand and beautiful, but they are not, as it were, in "striking distance"—not so located that the visiting stranger will be sure to see them.

Central Park, gentlemen, adorned by such an attraction as my brother and myself, and others after us, will furnish, and beautified by the care and intelligence of your excellent Board of Park Commissioners, will fill this void, and will supply, too, a playground and a breathing spot for your children and a place of gathering and recreation for those of our citizens who would like to see a stretch of green and a shady nook without taking a trip to Oldham or Bullitt County.

THE DEDICATION

The happy consummation of our plan was reached on November 9, 1901, when the statue was unveiled with impressive ceremonies in front of the Court House, this site having been selected in preference to Central Park. What transpired on this auspicious occasion is set forth, in the following account, which appeared in the *Courier-Journal* on the morning of the next day:

BEFORE AN ASSEMBLAGE OF PERSONS WHO NUMBERED FULLY 4,000, THE BRONZE STATUE OF THOMAS JEFFERSON, PRESIDENT, STATESMAN, PATRIOT, AND AUTHOR OF THE DECLARATION OF INDEPENDENCE, WAS UNVEILED.

THE STATUE WAS PRESENTED TO THE PEOPLE OF LOUISVILLE BY MESSRS. ISAAC W. AND BERNARD BERNHEIM, AND IS A WORK OF ART WHICH WILL STAND TO COMMEMORATE THE ILLUSTRIOUS JEFFERSON FOR YEARS TO COME. IT RESTS ON A RICH AND HEAVY BLOCK OF GRANITE, AND IS LOCATED ON JEFFERSON STREET, DIRECTLY IN FRONT OF THE COURT HOUSE. NEAR THE BASE OF THE STATUE PROPER, AND FACING THE CORINTHIAN COLUMNS OF THE COURT HOUSE, IS A FIGURE REPRESENTING JUSTICE. THIS FIGURE LOOKS TOWARD THE STATUE OF HENRY CLAY, KENTUCKY'S GREAT STATESMAN, WHICH STANDS IN THE CENTER OF THE BIG ROTUNDA OF THE COURT HOUSE. AFTER AN ELOQUENT ADDRESS BY FORMER GOV. W. O. BRADLEY, AND THE SINGING OF THE "STAR-SPANGLED BANNER" BY THE VAST CROWD, MISS ETHEL BERNHEIM, THE LITTLE SIX-YEAR-OLD DAUGHTER OF MR. B. BERNHEIM, PULLED THE CORD WHICH HELD THE WHITE CANVAS OVER THE BRONZE FIGURE. AT 12:59 O'CLOCK THE CANVAS WAS REMOVED FROM THE STATUE, THE SPECTATORS SAT SILENTLY, AND THE IMAGE OF JEFFERSON, CAST IN COLD METAL, STOOD OUT. THE KEENEST OBSERVER OF THIS PART OF THE CEREMONY WAS SIR MOSES EZEKIEL, THE SCULPTOR WHO MODELED THE STATUE AND THE FOUR FIGURES AT

ITS BASE. HE SAT LIKE ONE TRANSFIXED WHEN THE CLOTH SLIPPED FROM ITS FASTENINGS AND FELL IN A HEAP TO THE GROUND.

THERE WAS A SUDDEN BURST OF APPLAUSE. THE SCULPTOR'S BLACK EYES BRIGHTENED AND HE CHUCKLED WITH TRUE DELIGHT. IT WAS HIS WORK. HE HAD MADE THE FIGURE WITH HIS OWN HANDS. FROM MATERIAL WITHOUT SHAPE OR FORM HE HAD WROUGHT A LIKENESS, ALMOST PERFECT IN DETAIL, OF THOMAS JEFFERSON, AND THE APPLAUSE MEANT THAT HUNDREDS OF PEOPLE AROUND HIM APPROVED HIS WORK.

CROWD GATHERS ON THE SQUARE

LONG BEFORE TWELVE O'CLOCK, THE HOUR SET FOR THE UNVEILING, PEOPLE THRONGED JEFFERSON STREET BETWEEN FIFTH AND SIXTH. THEY EDGED THEIR WAY CLOSE TO THE STATUE, BUT THEY WERE KEPT BACK A REASONABLE DISTANCE BY A RAILING WHICH INCLOSED THE SEATS RETAINED FOR THE INVITED GUESTS. THE PLATFORM WAS GENEROUSLY DECORATED WITH THE NATIONAL COLORS. ON THE STAND WERE MANY OF THE MOST PROMINENT CITIZENS OF LOUISVILLE AND KENTUCKY. AMONG THEM WERE MAYOR CHARLES P. WEAVER, EX-GOVERNOR W. O. BRADLEY, JUDGE B. L. D. GUFFY, JUDGE GEORGE DURELLE, JUDGE STERLING B. TONEY, JUDGE JAMES P. GREGORY, JUDGE HENRY S. BARKER, EX-JUDGE J. WHEELER McGEE, R. C. KINKEAD, W. C. OWENS, SAMUEL GRABFELDER, AARON KOHN, JOSEPH SELLIGMAN, JOHN S. MORRIS, GEORGE D. TODD, WILLIAM THALHEIMER, E. H. MARK, JUDGE JOHN W. BARR, AND JAMES S. PIRTLE.

THE LOUISVILLE MILITARY BAND GAVE A CONCERT WHILE THE PEOPLE TOOK THEIR SEATS ON THE PLATFORM.

EXERCISES ARE OPENED

AT 12:05 O'CLOCK JUDGE JAMES S. PIRTLE CALLED THE GATHERING TO ORDER. HE SAID THAT THE STATUE WHICH WAS

TO BE UNVEILED WAS A MEMORIAL TO THOMAS JEFFERSON, WHO WAS ONE OF THE FIRST TO SPEAK OUT FOR FREEDOM AND EQUALITY OF MAN. HE SAID HE HOPED THE STATUE WOULD MAKE THE NAME OF JEFFERSON MORE SYNONYMOUS WITH THE WORDS, "LIBERTY, EQUALITY, AND FRATERNITY," AND WOULD SERVE AS AN INSPIRATION TO THE PEOPLE OF LOUISVILLE TO AID IN THE PRESERVATION OF THE GREAT PRINCIPLES OF THE GOVERNMENT WHICH HAD BEEN LAID BY THOMAS JEFFERSON. HE SAID THAT JEFFERSON'S FRAMING OF THE DECLARATION OF INDEPENDENCE, EVEN IF HE HAD DONE NOTHING MORE FOR HIS PEOPLE, WAS SUFFICIENT TO MAKE HIS NAME IMMORTAL.

RABBI H. G. ENELOW DELIVERED A PRAYER, AND THE PEOPLE STOOD AND SANG "AMERICA."

MR. BRADLEY'S ADDRESS

MR. PIRTLE INTRODUCED FORMER GOVERNOR BRADLEY BY SAYING THAT AS GOVERNOR OF KENTUCKY MR. BRADLEY HAD BEEN AN EMULATOR OF JEFFERSON.

THE SPEAKER BEGAN BY SAYING THAT HE DID NOT AGREE WITH JEFFERSON CONCERNING HIS POLICY AS TO CONSTITUTIONAL GOVERNMENT, BUT HE HAD COME TO PAY TRIBUTE TO THE WORKS OF THE MAN WHO HAD CONTRIBUTED, LARGELY IN MAKING AMERICA WHAT IT IS TODAY. ONE BY ONE HE RECORDED THE STATESMAN'S ACHIEVEMENTS. HE SAID HE COULD NOT SPEAK OF JEFFERSON'S ACCOMPLISHMENTS AS FOREIGN MINISTER OR PRESIDENT, BUT OF OTHER THINGS HE DID WHICH HE HIMSELF REGARDED AS WORTHY DEEDS. HE SAID THAT JEFFERSON HAD WRITTEN THE DECLARATION OF INDEPENDENCE, WHICH WAS THE MOST REMARKABLE AND THE GREATEST STATE PAPER KNOWN IN HISTORY. HE SAID THIS ONE ACT WAS ENOUGH TO IMMORTALIZE HIM AND MAKE AMERICANS REVERE HIS NAME AND MEMORY FOR ALL TIME TO COME.

OPPOSITION TO SLAVERY

HE WAS THE FIRST TO SPEAK OUT AGAINST SLAVERY AND TO SAY THAT THERE WAS NOTHING MORE CERTAIN IN THE BOOKS OF FATE THAN THAT SLAVERY COULD NOT LIVE. "IF PEOPLE HAD TAKEN JEFFERSON'S WORD, THE WAR COULD HAVE BEEN AVERTED AND THOUSANDS OF OUR BRAVEST AND BEST MEN SPARED."

HE SAID THAT JEFFERSON'S TEACHING IN FAVOR OF RELIGIOUS FREEDOM, FAIR AND IMPARTIAL TRIAL BY JURY, AND THE RULE OF THE MAJORITY, WERE THE GREAT AND UNDERLYING PRINCIPLES OF THE GOVERNMENT.

HE SAID THAT JEFFERSON WAS THE ORIGINATOR OF THE PUBLIC-SCHOOL SYSTEM OF THE UNITED STATES; IN FOUNDING THE UNIVERSITY OF VIRGINIA HE HAD DONE A NOBLE WORK..

MR. BERNHEIM'S GRATITUDE

MR. BRADLEY RELATED A CONVERSATION HE HAD HAD WITH MR. I. W. BERNHEIM WHEN HE WAS ASKED TO MAKE AN ADDRESS AT THE UNVEILING OF THE STATUE. SAID HE:

"I WILL DIGRESS A MOMENT TO RELATE A CONVERSATION WHICH OCCURRED BETWEEN ONE OF THE PATRIOTIC CITIZENS, WHO PRESENTED THIS SPLENDID STATUE TO THE CITY, AND MYSELF. SAID HE: 'I AT FIRST THOUGHT IT WOULD BE MOST APPROPRIATE TO PRESENT A STATUE OF ABRAHAM LINCOLN; BUT ON REFLECTION I WAS SATISFIED THAT HAVING BEEN A KENTUCKIAN HE WOULD MOST CERTAINLY BE FITLY REMEMBERED AT AN EARLY DAY. AFTER DELIBERATION, IT OCCURRED TO ME, THAT AS MY BROTHER AND I WERE FOREIGN BORN, HAD BEEN NATURALIZED IN AND PROTECTED BY THIS GOVERNMENT, AND UNDER ITS BENIGN RULE HAD ENJOYED SO MANY BLESSINGS, THAT IT WOULD BE A FITTING THING TO PRESENT THE STATUE OF HIM WHO HAD DONE MORE THAN ANY OTHER MAN TO MAKE THIS COUNTRY FREE, AND WHO HAD MADE OUR SUCCESS AND HAPPINESS POSSIBLE

BY INSPIRING AMERICANS WITH THE TRUTH AND JUSTICE OF THAT IMMORTAL DECLARATION, ALL MEN ARE CREATED EQUAL.' "

NAME CANNOT DIE

IN CONCLUSION, MR. BRADLEY SAID OF JEFFERSON:

"THOUGH DEAD, HE LIVES. HE LIVES THROUGH EXAMPLE; HE LIVES THROUGH HIS TEACHINGS; HE LIVES IN THE DECLARATION; HE LIVES IN THE GREAT UNIVERSITY; HE LIVES IN THE FREEDOM OF RELIGION; THE LIBERTY OF CONSCIENCE; THE ALL-EMBRACING FREEDOM THAT NOW BLESSES THE PEOPLE OF THIS COUNTRY, AND HE LIVES IN THE HEARTS AND MINDS OF HIS COUNTRYMEN. HIS IS INDEED ONE OF THE FEW IMMORTAL NAMES THAT WERE NOT BORN TO DIE."

THE STATUE WAS THEN UNVEILED AND BATTERY A FIRED A SALUTE.

MAYOR WEAVER ACCEPTS STATUE

AFTER THE SINGING OF THE "STAR-SPANGLED BANNER" CHAIRMAN PIRTLE INTRODUCED MAYOR WEAVER, SAYING IT SHOULD BE A SOURCE OF GREAT PLEASURE TO MR. WEAVER, AT THE CLOSE OF A SUCCESSFUL ADMINISTRATION AS MAYOR, TO RECEIVE AS THE CITY'S OWN SUCH A BEAUTIFUL PIECE OF ART. THE MAYOR MADE A SHORT SPEECH, IN WHICH HE COMPLIMENTED SIR MOSES EZEKIEL'S GENIUS AND SPOKE OF THE GENEROUS SPIRIT MANIFESTED BY THE MESSRS. BERNHEIM IN MAKING SUCH A GIFT TO THE CITY. HE SAID THAT THEIR EXAMPLE WAS WELL WORTHY OF EMULATION. ON BEHALF OF THE PEOPLE OF THE CITY, HE ACCEPTED THE STATUE AND THANKED THE DONORS FOR IT.

CRIES FOR EZEKIEL

There were cries for Ezekiel. The sculptor mounted the platform and was presented by Mr. Pirtle. Someone said "Speech!" and Mr. Ezekiel heard what he said. He immediately sprang from the platform and ran over to a seat in the inclosure, where he hid himself behind the broad shoulders of Mayor Weaver and Mr. Bradley.

There were also cries for Mr. I. W. Bernheim, but he motioned to the bandmaster to strike up "My Old Kentucky Home." The big crowd stood as one person and sang the melody. The benediction was then pronounced by Rabbi Enelow.

EDITORIAL COMMENT

Not in any sense of vanity, but to emphasize the fact that our gift was received in the spirit in which it was given, I reproduce the editorial comments on the Commercial Club reception. One is from the *Louisville Dispatch*, and is as follows:

Commercial Club Meeting

Louisville is fortunate in having such citizens as the Bernheim Brothers. The address delivered at the Commercial Club by Mr. I. W. Bernheim yesterday marks him as a student and a thinker as well as a successful business man. In a gift of a statue of Jefferson he displays great liberality, a recognition of his wealth as a public trust, and an appreciation of the life-principle of American civilization and progress as exemplified by the life and work of the man whose memory he would honor. The proposition to donate a sum of money to provide prizes for essays on national characters and events by pupils of the public schools, as a means of cultivating patriotism and an interest in public affairs, is no less commendable than the gift of the statue of the foremost statesman of the age.

The other is from the *Courier-Journal*, and reads:

A Pleasant New Year's Meeting

The New Year's gathering of the Commercial Club was a peculiarly pleasant occasion. The testimonial to the Messrs. Bernheim in consideration of their donation of a statue of Thomas Jefferson to the city was in the spirit of Thomas Jefferson himself. The Commercial Club is a democratic organization in every sense and welcomes all to its membership, provided only they are willing to aid in its work.

It is a fact worthy of note that both last year and this time the election to honorary membership was of an adoptive citizen. Mr. Charles H. Shackleton, who first received this testimonial, like Mr. Isaac W. Bernheim, was not a Kentuckian and came to this city about a score of years ago. He was not a wealthy merchant, and though he filled a large and useful part in Louisville's commercial life, he had nothing to give to the Club's work beyond his time and the suggestions of a fruitful mind. Mr. Bernheim has devoted time and talents to public movements, and, in addition, has been able to share the gifts of fortune with the city. Both men are equally honored, for each has done according to his ability, and they are conspicuous examples of the class of citizens the principles of Jefferson have drawn to our shores.

Mr. Bernheim in his remarks took occasion to urge renewed efforts to secure Central Park for the city. Assuredly this must be done, and we must also have a free library. The Commercial Club has pledged its influence to these objects of public interest. What was said and done at yesterday's meeting will help along this and every other movement which tends to make this a greater and better city, adding not only to its wealth and population, but also to its culture.

My tale is finished. It has wound along through sunlit highways and through valleys where sometimes shadows lurked. Yet every hardship that I endured has left me not only richer or wiser in human experience and knowledge, but has helped to equip me with the health, vigor, and strength that now enables me to so sturdily and resolutely enter upon the autumn of life.

APPENDIX

[*THE REPUBLIC,* ST. LOUIS, WEDNESDAY,

APRIL 17, 1895.]

ADVOCATE TEMPERANCE

POSITION OF THE DEALERS IN LIQUORS STATED—SECOND ANNUAL CONVENTION OF THE NATIONAL WINE AND SPIRIT DEALERS' ASSOCIATION—SALOONS ARE THE AMERICAN WORKMEN'S CLUBS— BUSINESS BEFORE THE MEETING.

The second annual convention of the National Wine and Spirit Dealers' Association was called to order by President I. W. Bernheim, of Louisville, Ky., at 10 o'clock Tuesday morning, in the assembly room of the St. Nicholas Hotel. Over one hundred delegates were present. President Bernheim's opening remarks were as follows:

GENTLEMEN: IT IS A SOURCE OF GREAT PLEASURE TO GREET SO LARGE AN ATTENDANCE UPON THIS, THE SECOND ANNUAL MEETING OF THE NATIONAL WINE AND SPIRIT ASSOCIATION.

THE NATIONAL WINE AND SPIRIT ASSOCIATION HAS, THANKS TO THE EFFICIENT SERVICES OF THE SECRETARY AND THE DEVOTION TO DUTY OF THE BOARD OF CONTROL, INSTITUTED SOME MEASURES WHICH HAVE PROVEN BENEFICIAL. IT HAS ATTEMPTED SOME REFORMS WHICH, I REGRET TO SAY, HAVE NOT FULLY MATERIALIZED, AND SET IN MOTION OTHERS WHICH MAY PROVE OF GREAT VALUE.

THE UNSOLICITED PRICE LIST, WITH ITS BANEFUL AND MISCHIEVOUS INFLUENCE, RECEIVED CAREFUL ATTENTION, AND THAT THE EFFORTS TO SUPPRESS IT HAVE ONLY BEEN

PARTIALLY SUCCESSFUL IS IN A MEASURE DUE TO THE NEW CONDITIONS PRODUCED BY THE ADVANCE OF THE INTERNAL REVENUE TAX AND THE EXTENSION OF THE BONDED PERIOD. SETTLED VALUES, A STEADY MARKET, AND ABOVE ALL A BETTER UNDERSTANDING AMONGST OURSELVES, MAY IN TIME PRODUCE A FULL REALIZATION OF OUR EFFORTS.

THE PROHIBITIONISTS (OF THE OLD SCHOOL) HAVE CHANGED THE THEATER OF WAR FROM THE EAST AND WEST TO THE SOUTH. THE EAST AND WEST HAVE BEEN TAUGHT BY BITTER EXPERIENCE THAT TOTAL PROHIBITION BY STATUTORY ENACTMENTS INVARIABLY RESULTS IN THE TRANSFER OF THE TRADE FROM THE WELL-REGULATED, LAWFULLY LICENSED SALOON, MANAGED AND OPERATED BY THE LAW-ABIDING, RESPONSIBLE CITIZEN, TO THAT OF THE BOOTLEGGER AND MOONSHINER, WHO IS EVER READY FOR THE SAKE OF GAIN TO DISREGARD ALIKE THE LAWS OF THE STATE AND OF THE UNITED STATES.

IOWA HAS LATELY ENACTED PARTLY A LICENSE SYSTEM; KANSAS IS RIPE FOR RESUBMISSION; NORTH DAKOTA WILL, AT ITS NEXT STATE ELECTION, TAKE A VOTE ON THE REPEAL OF THE CONSTITUTIONAL PROHIBITION. EVEN ONE OF THE BANNER STATES OF PROHIBITION—THE STATE OF NEW HAMPSHIRE—SHOWS SIGNS OF REAWAKENING, AND IS GIVING STRONG EVIDENCE THAT THE LAWMAKERS RECOGNIZE THE TRUISM THAT THE WORLD CANNOT BE LEGISLATED INTO AN EARTHLY PARADISE, AFTER THE OLD PRECONCEIVED NOTION OF THE POLITICAL PROHIBITIONIST. IT IS NEEDLESS TO REASSERT THE PRINCIPLE WHICH HAS EVER SERVED US AS A GUIDE.

THE NATIONAL WINE AND SPIRIT ASSOCIATION IS NEITHER THE FRIEND NOR ADVOCATE OF INTEMPERANCE; IT FAVORS A FAIR LICENSE LAW WHICH WILL PLACE THE RETAIL TRADE IN THE HANDS OF LAW-ABIDING CITIZENS, AND MAKE THE SALOON NOT AN EVIL, AS MANY CONSIDER IT, OR AN INSTITUTION TO BE APOLOGIZED FOR, AS A LARGE PORTION OF OUR TRADE CONCEIVE IT TO BE, BUT RATHER A MOST

IMPORTANT FACTOR IN THE DEVELOPMENT OF OUR COMPLEX AND SURGING CIVILIZATION. IN A WORD, THE SALOON SHOULD BECOME THE WORKINGMAN'S CLUB IN THE FULL SENSE, AND IT SHOULD BE SO CONDUCTED AS TO MAKE HIM HAPPIER, BETTER, AND MORE PROSPEROUS AND PATRIOTIC BECAUSE OF ITS EXISTENCE AND OF HIS CONTACT WITH IT.

OUR ASSOCIATION HAS SHOWN DURING THE PAST YEAR A HEALTHY INCREASE IN MEMBERSHIP. ITS FINANCES ARE IN GOOD CONDITION.

THE NECESSITY OF COOPERATION IN WARDING OFF HOSTILE LEGISLATION, THE DEVISING OF MEANS TO LESSEN LOSSES IN THE CONDUCT OF OUR BUSINESS, THE SIMPLIFYING OF THE INTERNAL REVENUE LAWS, WITHOUT IN THE SLIGHTEST DEGREE DECREASING THEIR EFFICIENCY, ARE MEASURES WHICH MIGHT BE DISCUSSED DURING OUR MEETING WITH PROFIT.

On motion, the chair was instructed to appoint a committee of five to which all resolutions and suggestions as to the welfare of the trade should be submitted without debate, and also a committee of five to examine the books of the Secretary and Treasurer, and report at the afternoon session.

George G. Brown, of Kentucky, then read a paper on "The Relation of Manufacturers and Tenders of Alcoholic Stimulants to Society."

After the reading of Mr. Brown's paper the President announced the appointment of H. Van Nes, A. C. Sellner, George G. Brown, S. Wertheimer, and M. Eppstein as the Committee on Resolutions, with instructions to report at the afternoon session. The meeting then adjourned until 3 p. m.

Upon reconvening in the afternoon the Convention was declared to be in executive session, and all present except members were excluded. It was said after the adjournment for the day that the executive session had been devoted to the discussion of the reports of the committees appointed during the forenoon, the nature of which could not be learned, and the general discussion of business.

At the session to be held this morning the election of officers for the ensuing year will be held. The Convention will adjourn *sine die* about noon, and the members will devote the afternoon to sight-seeing and the reception of courtesies tendered by the local members of the Association. Tonight an elaborate banquet will be spread by the St. Louis members in honor of the visiting delegates, in the banqueting hall of the St. Nicholas.

[*THE COURIER-JOURNAL,* LOUISVILLE,
WEDNESDAY, JANUARY 1, 1896.]

NEW BUILDING

Y. M. H. A. WILL CELEBRATE THIS EVENING—MESSRS. BERNHEIM'S GIFT—TODAY ALSO MARKS THE ASSOCIATION'S FIFTH ANNIVERSARY.

The handsome new building of the Young Men's Hebrew Association, on the east side of First Street, south of Walnut, will be dedicated tonight with proper ceremonies.

At the same time the Association celebrates the fifth anniversary of the completion of its gymnasium and the beginning of its active usefulness.

The Association was organized in the year 1890, and had its origin in the philanthropic designs of Mr. I. W. Bernheim, the first President of the Association, and who has continued ever since in that office. Through the generous assistance and hearty cooperation of the best and most influential Jewish citizens, the money was raised with which to purchase a lot 50x250 feet, on First Street, running through to East Street, and to erect thereon a complete gymnasium. The gymnasium hall was finished in the latter part of 1890, and was dedicated January 1, 1891. It is admitted to be one of the best fitted and most modern gymnasiums with baths in the city of Louisville. Its equipments are of the best and most approved character. At its head has been a succession of competent instructors. Professor Gearhart has been in charge for two years, and is such a universal favorite with the members that there is no doubt that he will be re-elected for the next year. The classes are large and enthusiastic and are doing as good all-round work as is being done in any of the gymnasiums in the city. In the rear of the gymnasium is a large lot, used for a running track and outdoor exercises during the summer. Lights are provided at night, so that during the heated period it is not necessary to suspend the exercises of the gymnasium.

The building that is to be dedicated tonight has been heretofore fully described. It is the design of Messrs. Clarke & Loomis, of this city, and is in the style of the Italian Renaissance, of stone, pressed brick and terra cotta, with plate-glass windows. The main entrance is approached from the street by a wide flight of stone steps, with massive stone coping and pediments and granitoid walk in the yard from the steps to the vestibule. The vestibule floor is tiled and has marble wainscoting. One enters through rich but plain beveled plate-glass doors, in keeping with the design of the front. On the right of the center main hall is the parlor, 16x26 feet; on the left the reception room, 16x17, and back of the reception room is the stair hall, with its oak staircase, and the toilet rooms. From this hall is also an entrance into the large gymnasium room.

The second story has a library 16 ½x21 feet, and an adjoining study room 21x26 feet. These two rooms and hall can be thrown into one by means of large sliding doors.

The third floor is devoted to club or lodge purposes, and has the required ante-room necessary for their convenience and mysteries.

The interior is of natural wood finish. The building is heated by steam, lighted by electricity, and has all the latest improved fittings and modern conveniences.

This building is the gift of Mr. I. W. Bernheim and Mr. Bernard Bernheim. The handsome furnishings of the building were paid for by the proceeds of the bazaar recently given at Music Hall for the benefit of the Association.

During the past five years, although not thoroughly equipped for that purpose, the Young Men's Hebrew Association has not lost sight of the greater work that it had intended to do. A series of successful monthly literary entertainments have been given in the Gymnasium Hall. Upon the programmes were lectures upon various historical, popular, and scientific subjects. Dr. Adolph Moses, who has had charge of this department, fixed a high standard of excellence that has never been departed from. Taken all in all, the series of lectures delivered at this institution during its history have excited attention for their merit and for the interest that the members have taken in them.

The musical entertainments, although given as adjuncts to the lectures, have always been among its pleasant features. Contrary to the course usually adopted in such institutions, those in charge of the musical part of the programme have endeavored to avoid making it the means of showing off infant prodigies or rank amateurs, but, on the contrary, have sought and succeeded in obtaining the services of people recognized in their particular line as artists.

The Association, in spite of its name, is strictly non-sectarian. There is no qualification required for admission to membership except that the applicant must be of good moral character, and must come properly recommended. The present membership of the Association is about three hundred and fifty and just now is experiencing quite a boom. While the majority of the members are of Jewish birth, a large proportion are Christians. The position that this Association has taken upon this matter has attracted no little attention. In response to the question as to what purpose the Young Men's Hebrew Association could have in inviting Gentiles into its membership, the Secretary said:

IT WAS PRIMARILY THE DESIRE ON OUR PART TO CULTIVATE A CLOSER AND MORE INTIMATE PERSONAL AND SOCIAL RELATIONSHIP WITH OUR FELLOW CITIZENS. WE COULD SEE NO REASON FOR NOT INVITING THEM. IN OUR BUSINESS LIFE WE MEET ALL OUR FELLOW CITIZENS WITH THE VERY HAPPIEST RESULTS, BUT THIS HAS BEEN CARRIED ONLY TO A LIMITED DEGREE INTO OUR SOCIAL LIFE. THOSE IN CHARGE OF THE POLICY OF THE ASSOCIATION FELT THAT THIS WAS UNFORTUNATE, AND THAT THERE OUGHT TO BE NO DISTINCTION BETWEEN JEW AND GENTILE IN OUR SOCIAL RELATIONS. WE OBJECTED TO THE IDEA OF ANYTHING IN THE WAY OF A SOCIAL OR PERSONAL CLUB THAT SHOULD BE DISTINCTLY FOR OUR OWN PEOPLE. WE, THEREFORE, INVITED, AND STILL INVITE, ALL WHO ARE QUALIFIED BY CHARACTER

AND STANDING, JEW OR GENTILE, TO JOIN US. WE WANT OUR CHRISTIAN AND JEWISH YOUNG MEN TO MEET IN A SOCIAL WAY AT ONE PLACE, AT LEAST, WHERE THEY COULD LEARN TO APPRECIATE THAT BOTH WERE ENDOWED WITH THE SAME VIRTUES, WITH THE SAME WEAKNESSES, THAT EACH ARE FASHIONED IN A SIMILAR MOLD, THAT THE UNFORTUNATE PREJUDICES OF MANY YEARS, NOW HAPPILY PASSING AWAY, WERE BUILT UPON FICTION, AND THAT THERE IS NO NATURAL ANTAGONISM. ENMITIES BASED ON PREJUDICES WE BELIEVE MUST PASS AWAY BEFORE A BETTER MUTUAL UNDERSTANDING THAT PROVES SUCH PREJUDICES TO BE UNFOUNDED. OUR EXPERIMENT HAS HAPPILY BEEN A MOST SUCCESSFUL ONE, AND WE FEEL EVERY ENCOURAGEMENT TO CONTINUE AS WE HAVE BEGUN.

Of the future of the Association there can be no doubt. It possesses a handsome building, containing reception and reading rooms, together with its gymnasium, altogether its property costing in the neighborhood of $20,000, with a sufficient membership to assure its continued usefulness.

The officers of the Association at this time are: I. W. Bernheim, President; Norton L. Goldsmith, Vice-president; Henry Levy, Treasurer; Alfred Selligman, Recording Secretary, and S. Kaufman, Custodian of Buildings and Financial Secretary.

The directors of the Association are: Bernard Bernheim, J. B. Washer, Fred Levy, Joseph Cohen, Siegel Bonner, Henry Bakrow, and Isadore Rosenbaum. All of the officers are *ex officio* directors.

The dedication services tonight will be of the most interesting character. All members of the Association and their friends are invited to be present. The programme will include an opening prayer by Dr. A. Moses; an address, "Trade as a Profession," by Mr. Abraham Flexner, and remarks by the Rev. S. M. Hamilton.

[*THE TIMES,* LOUISVILLE,
WEDNESDAY, JANUARY 15, 1896.]

BANQUETED

TESTIMONIAL TO THE BERNHEIM
BROTHERS
BY THE Y. M. H. A.

With words of profound gratitude and to the music of clinking glasses, the Board of Directors and the members of the various committees of the Y. M. H. A. last night showed their appreciation of the efforts of Messrs. I. W. and B. Bernheim in behalf of the Association. The testimonial was in the nature of a banquet, which was given at the Galt House. The menu was elaborate and sufficient to satisfy the most fastidious. Mr. B. Bernheim was detained at home by sickness.

Mr. D. I. Heyman presided gracefully as toastmaster. After the dinner had been disposed of, toasts were in order. Every one present was called on, and none failed to respond. Mr. I. W. Bernheim made a very graceful speech. The decorations at the table were green and red. Mr. Bernheim leaves January 23d on an extended European trip, and the glasses clinked the last time to a "bon voyage." Those present were: Messrs. Dolf Wile, Barney Dreyfus, Henry Balcrow, Henry Levy, B. F. Washer, S. Bronner, Fred Levy, Dr. A. Moses, Charles Weinstock, William Rosenberg, Maxwell Davis, M. H. Florsheim, Sam Greenbaum, Joseph Cohen, D. Davis, Jesse Sickles, J. B. Washer, D. I. Heyman, Robert Marcus, A. L. Dembitz, Julius Barkhouse, Alfred Selligman, and I. F. Marcosson.

[*THE TIMES*, LOUISVILLE,
TUESDAY, MAY 12, 1896.]

WORK OF A YEAR

COMMERCIAL CLUB'S PROGRESS OF THE PAST TWELVE MONTHS REVIEWED—MR. I. W. BERNHEIM ELECTED HONORARY MEMBER FOR THIS YEAR.

At the annual meeting of the Commercial Club, held at the Board of Trade today, Secretary Thomas P. Craig read the ninth annual report of the Secretary of the Club. In starting he said that, while the Club had not put through any gigantic schemes during the year, it had been far from idle. The work done had been chiefly in the way of entertainment. The Club assisted in entertaining the G.A.R., and had done in this connection a great deal of advertising for the city; had entertained the Indiana Editorial Association, and had, with the Board of Trade, sent a business men's excursion to the Atlanta Exposition.

During the year delegates were sent from the Club to a number of important meetings. The Club had headed a movement to secure from the Legislature a reform in the matter of municipal taxation, and also one to have Louisville put on the same footing with other cities in regard to exempting new manufacturing enterprises from taxation.

During the year the Club gained in membership forty-one, and lost by resignation, suspension, etc., one hundred and seven, leaving the membership at the end of the year four hundred. Many of those lost, however, will be reinstated shortly.

The financial statement showed the Club to be in a good condition. The present administration has carried out its resolve to live within the income derived from dues and fees. The receipts during the year were $2,099.63 and disbursements $1,793.10, leaving a balance in the treasury of $306.53.

The Secretary referred to the fact that Louisville is rapidly becoming a leading convention city, and cited the various bodies which will meet this year, and which, it is estimated, will bring one hundred thousand strangers to the city.

The Secretary regretted that the Merchants' and Manufacturers' Association, organized some years ago, has not been given proper support by the wholesale merchants. In order for the city to increase or even hold her present trade, she should be more liberal in the distribution of free transportation.

When the time came for announcing the name of the public-spirited citizen on whom had been conferred the distinction of honorary member for the year, Mr. Maxwell Davis, one of the retiring directors, addressed the meeting as follows:

MR. CHAIRMAN AND GENTLEMEN: THERE IS NOTHING, IN MY JUDGMENT, THAT SO MUCH INDICATES THE PROGRESS AND WELL-BEING OF A CITY AS DOES THE NUMBER OF ITS ENTERPRISING AND PUBLIC- SPIRITED RESIDENTS. THEIR PRESENCE LENDS AN AIR OF PROSPERITY AND BESPEAKS THE ATTRACTIVENESS OF THE PLACE. AS EMERSON SAYS: "IF THERE WERE ANY MAGNET THAT WOULD POINT TO THE COUNTRIES AND HOUSES WHERE ARE THE PERSONS WHO ARE INTRINSICALLY RICH AND POWERFUL, I WOULD SELL ALL AND BUY IT AND PUT MYSELF ON THE ROAD TODAY. THE RACE GOES WITH US ON THEIR CREDITS. THE KNOWLEDGE THAT IN THE CITY IS A MAN WHO INVENTED THE RAILROAD RAISES THE CREDIT OF ALL THE CITIZENS. BUT ENORMOUS POPULATIONS, IF THEY BE BEGGARS, ARE DISGUSTING, LIKE A MOVING CHEESE, LIKE HILLS OF ANTS, OR FLEAS—THE MORE THE WORSE." AND SO, WHEN THE COMMERCIAL CLUB WAS ORGANIZED, WITH THE SOLE PURPOSE OF PROMOTING THE WELFARE OF THE CITY, RECOGNIZING THE TRUTH OF THIS, FOR THE PURPOSE OF STIMULATING INTEREST IN ITS WORK, AND TO ACCORD DUE RECOGNITION TO SUCH AS HAVE WELL SERVED ITS PURPOSES, IT WAS ENACTED THAT EACH YEAR THE DIRECTORY SHOULD SELECT AS AN HONORARY MEMBER ONE MAN, PRE-EMINENT BY HIGH ABILITY AND HIGH CHARACTER, THEIR OBJECT BEING, AS I HAVE STATED, NOT ONLY TO ENLIVEN AN INTEREST IN

THE COMMERCIAL CLUB, BUT TO EXCITE IN EACH AND EVERY CITIZEN AN INTEREST IN THE WELFARE OF HIS CITY, WHICH IS SYNONYMOUS WITH THE OBJECTS OF THE ORGANIZATION. IT IS, THEREFORE, THE DUTY OF THE DIRECTORY, IN MAKING THE SELECTION OF THE PERSON UPON WHOM THIS HONOR IS TO BE CONFERRED, TO CONSIDER WHO THERE IS THAT HAS ESPECIALLY DISTINGUISHED HIMSELF BY ACTS OF BENEFICENCE, BY PUBLIC SPIRIT, AND BY AN EXHIBITION OF A LIVELY INTEREST IN THE WORKINGS OF THIS CLUB.

IT IS PROPER THAT I SHOULD SAY, AND I SUPPOSE THAT THE SAME HAS AND ALWAYS WILL BE THE CASE, THAT MORE THAN ONE NAME CAME TO THE NOTICE OF YOUR DIRECTORY, FOR I AM PROUD TO SAY THAT THERE HAVE ALWAYS BEEN IN OUR CITY MANY MEN READY AND WILLING TO USE THEIR TIME AND THEIR MEANS TO FURTHER THE GENERAL WELFARE OF THE COMMUNITY IN WHICH THEY LIVE. THIS WAS PARTICULARLY TRUE THIS YEAR, AND WHEN WE FINALLY DETERMINED UPON THE GENTLEMAN WHOSE NAME I WILL PRESENTLY MENTION, WE ALL REALIZED THAT HE, ABOVE ALMOST ANY ONE ELSE IN OUR CITY, HAS BEEN ONE OF THE MOST FAITHFUL, MOST WILLING, MOST READY OF THE SERVANTS OF THE COMMERCIAL CLUB TO DO ITS BIDDINGS AND TO GRANT ITS ASKINGS. A MAN WHO IS PUBLIC-SPIRITED BECAUSE HE LOVES TO BE; IS CHARITABLE BECAUSE IT GIVES HIM PLEASURE TO DEAL WITH THAT WHICH HE HAS BEEN ENDOWED, AS IT WAS INTENDED THAT HE SHOULD. APPROPRIATELY CAN BE APPLIED TO HIM THE LINES: "HE WHO WELL HAS SERVED HIS COUNTRY AND HIS COUNTRY'S WEALTH DESERVED." I NEED BUT MENTION HIS NAME TO HAVE YOU BEAR ME OUT WHEN I SAY THAT THE TIME HAS NOT BEEN WHEN HE HAS BEEN CALLED UPON FOR HIS SERVICE, HIS COUNSEL OR HIS MONEY, BUT THAT HE HAS RESPONDED CHEERFULLY, LIBERALLY, AND READILY. THE COMMERCIAL CLUB IS TO BE CONGRATULATED THAT WE HAVE AS ONE OF OUR MEMBERS A MAN SO THOROUGHLY AT HEART IN CONSONANCE WITH EVERY MOVEMENT AND EVERY SUGGESTION MADE BY IT; AND A MAN WHO, HAVING LARGE PERSONAL INTERESTS, HAS NEVER YET FAILED TO RECOGNIZE

THIS ORGANIZATION AND ITS VALUE TO HIM AS ONE OF ITS CITIZENS. I AM HAPPY TO ANNOUNCE TO YOU, GENTLEMEN, THAT THE PERSON UPON WHOM WE CONFER THIS HONOR TODAY IS MR. I. W. BERNHEIM. (APPLAUSE.)

Then turning to Mr. Bernheim, Mr. Davis continued:

MR. BERNHEIM: IT IS WITH EXTREME PLEASURE THAT I CAN STATE TO YOU, AS A REPRESENTATIVE OF THE DIRECTORY, THAT ALTHOUGH THERE WERE SEVERAL FAVORITES, YET, WHEN IT WAS ANNOUNCED THAT YOU HAD RECEIVED THE REQUISITE NUMBER OF VOTES DETERMINING YOU AS THE PERSON ELECTED, IT WAS WITH AN EQUANIMITY THAT BUT BESPEAKS THE HIGH ESTEEM IN WHICH YOU ARE HELD BY YOUR FELLOW CITIZENS, THAT EACH AND EVERY MEMBER OF OUR DIRECTORY AGREED THAT THE HONOR HAD BEEN WELL PLACED. MAY IT BE THE GOOD FORTUNE OF SUCCEEDING DIRECTORIES TO DETERMINE UPON A MAN WHO IS SO GENERALLY RECOGNIZED AS ONE WHO PROPERLY BELONGS ON THE ROLL OF HONOR AMONG THE PUBLIC-SPIRITED CITIZENS. (LONG APPLAUSE.)

[*THE TIMES*, LOUISVILLE,
WEDNESDAY, DECEMBER 27, 1899.]

DEAL CLOSED

THE BERNHEIMS NOW OWN THE BAMBERGER-BLOOM BUILDING.

The deal to purchase the Bamberger-Bloom building, which the Messrs. Bernheim have had on for several weeks, has been closed. The purchase price is reported as $75,000 cash. The building belonged to the New York Life Insurance Company. It is six stories high and has a frontage of forty-six and one-half feet on Main Street and seventy-eight feet on Seventh Street. The Bernheims will remodel their purchase inside and use it for their whisky business. The building now occupied by them will be sold. Mr. Lithgow Smith, of the Columbia Finance and Trust Company, negotiated the deal.

[*THE COURIER-JOURNAL,* LOUISVILLE,
SUNDAY, DECEMBER 15, 1901.]

I. W. BERNHEIM, DISTILLER

SENIOR MEMBER OF BERNHEIM BROS, STARTED WITHOUT A PENNY, NOW WEALTHY; MEMBER OF BOARD OF TRADE, DONOR OF JEFFERSON STATUE TO CITY OF LOUISVILLE

In reply to the above questions, I beg to say that the successful man usually possesses three qualities in a marked degree—industry coupled with good health, capacity, and honesty.

Industry implies steady application and singleness of purpose. The old theory that change of pasture makes fat cattle may hold good in farming, but in business, with slight exceptions, it leads most always to failure.

With capacity must be combined an absolute faith in the correctness of one's own judgment and the necessary self-confidence to be guided by it.

Honesty is the banking capital of the struggling young man; his character and reputation must be jealously guarded and maintained. I have seen the morally weak and the dishonestly inclined sooner or later come to grief.

Wealth, in my humble opinion, is not a thing of luck, or the result of a deliberate and carefully fought campaign of industry, but rather the good judgment to take advantage, at the right time, of opportunities when they present themselves.

The present day and time offer greater opportunities to make fortunes than any previous period in the history of our country.

A population of seventy-five million of people, each with a purchasing and consuming capacity greater than that of the individual in any other country, Australia excepted, offers at home opportunities undreamed of a generation ago. Add to this, possibilities in our newly acquired territories, the opening up to civilization of Siberia and China, and the consequent drafts on American manufactures, on American labor, and on American enterprise and capital, and it requires no prophet to foretell that we will, in the course of a comparatively short period of years, face a financial and commercial activity which will greatly overmatch our present gratifying results. Our young men will participate in this glorious future, they will share in our increasing state of prosperity, and naturally will be the builders of great fortunes. Let us hope, however, that while striving for riches, they will not forget the teachings of the fathers of our glorious country, but uphold and guard jealously our republican principles, because our free institutions have made our prosperity a possibility, and without them there can be neither progress nor happiness.

[*THE COURIER-JOURNAL,*
LOUISVILLE, THURSDAY, MAY 1, 1902.]

GIVE BONDS

MESSRS. BERNHEIM PROVIDE FOR MAINTAINING STATUE—INCOME ABOUT $350 A YEAR—PRIZES FOR BEST ESSAYS ON THOMAS JEFFERSON—THE TRUSTEES ARE NAMED.

A deed of trust will be recorded in the County Clerk's office this morning which will convey from Messrs. Isaac W. and Bernard Bernheim ten city bonds, known as "forty-year 3 ½ percent refunding gold bonds, due July 1, 1941," to a board of trustees. The income from these bonds will be used in the maintenance of the statue of Thomas Jefferson, in front of the courthouse, and providing a prize or prizes annually for the best essay written by a pupil or pupils of the public schools commemorative of some national event or character connected with the life and times of Mr. Jefferson. The deed also provides for a prize for someone selected by the trustees who shall read annually on July 4, at the base of the statue, the Declaration of Independence. The bonds are of the face value of $10,000, but are worth about $11,000. The income will not be less than $350 a year.

The trustees who were appointed by the Messrs. Bernheim are as follows: D. I. Heyman, lawyer; E. W. Hays, banker; James S. Pirtle, lawyer; Abraham Flexner, educator; Thomas J. Wood, banker; W. O. Bradley, lawyer, and Alfred Selligman, lawyer. They met yesterday afternoon and organized as follows: D. I. Heyman, President; Alfred Selligman, Secretary; Thomas J. Wood, Abraham Flexner, and D. I. Heyman, committee to draft bylaws. The bonds have been turned over to the trustees and are deposited in a box in a safety vault, as provided in the deed.

The deed explains the action of the Messrs. Bernheim, as follows: "The first parties have lately presented to the city of Louisville a statue in bronze of Thomas Jefferson by Sir Moses Ezekiel, which has been erected upon the site selected for it in front of the courthouse of Jefferson County, Kentucky, and desire, in order to fully carry into effect their plans in relation to said statue, to establish a permanent fund for the uses and purposes and upon the trusts herein declared.''

The deed empowers the trustees to dispose of the bonds at any time, but the proceeds must be reinvested in city or United States bonds.

The following relates to the use of the income:

THE INCOME OF SAID TRUST FUND, OR SO MUCH THEREOF AS THE BOARD MAY DEEM NECESSARY OR APPROPRIATE, SHALL BE APPLIED BY SAID BOARD AS FOLLOWS:

FIRST—TO THE MAINTENANCE OF SAID STATUE, ITS BASE, AND THE RAILING AROUND IT, IN GOOD ORDER AND CONDITION.

SECOND—TO AN AWARD BY THE BOARD OR A MAJORITY OF ITS MEMBERS ON THE 4TH DAY OF JULY IN EACH YEAR OF A PRIZE OR PRIZES TO THOSE PUPILS OF THE PUBLIC SCHOOLS OF THE CITY OF LOUISVILLE, WITHOUT DISCRIMINATION AS TO THEIR RACE, COLOR, RELIGION, OR CONDITION, WHO SHALL PREPARE THE BEST ESSAY OR ESSAYS COMMEMORATIVE OF SOME NATIONAL EVENT OR CHARACTER CONNECTED WITH THE LIFE AND TIMES OF THOMAS JEFFERSON, AND TO THE ANNUAL SELECTION BY THE BOARD OF SOME SUITABLE PERSON, AN INHABITANT OF THE CITY OF LOUISVILLE, TO WHOM THE BOARD, IF IT SEES FIT, MAY ALSO AWARD A PRIZE, AND WHO SHALL, ON THAT DAY, PUBLICLY READ THE DECLARATION OF INDEPENDENCE AT THE BASE OF SAID STATUE, THE SAME TO BE ACCOMPANIED BY SUCH OTHER APPROPRIATE CEREMONIES AS THE BOARD MAY DEEM FIT.

Vacancies among the trustees shall be filled by the other members. The deed provides that the trustees shall elect a President and a Secretary and any officers they may see fit.

Mr. Heyman said yesterday afternoon that it is the intention of the trustees, if not too near vacation, to offer prizes for essays this year, as provided by the deed. The trustees will arrange for reading the Declaration of Independence and appropriate exercises at the base of the statue on July 4.

[TELEGRAM, JANUARY 15, 1907.]

Lipman Levy, Secretary,
Convention Hall,
Atlanta, Ga.

The construction of a modern college complete in its appointments will mark an epoch in the history of progressive American Israel. It will prove that reform has taken deep root, and will enable it to blossom and bear fruit, all for the greater glory of God and the rejuvenation of his people. You may announce, should you deem it proper, my readiness to defray the expense of the library building should the Council decide to proceed with the college construction.

Isaac W. Bernheim.

[TELEGRAM, ATLANTA, GA.,
JANUARY 17, 1907.]

I. W. Bernheim,
Palm Beach.

The Twentieth Council, on its own behalf and on behalf of the entire Union of American Hebrew Congregations, tenders you its sincere and profound thanks for your generous gift of a library building, which will so materially help to build up our great institution, and prays that you may witness the realization of your fondest hopes for all that is near and dear to your heart.

Adolph Kraus, President.
Lipman Levy, Secretary.

[*THE CINCINNATI ENQUIRER,*
JANUARY 17, 1907.]

PLANNED HOME OF HEBREW CONGREGATIONS

Within a short time work will be started on a series of buildings for the home of the Union of American Hebrew Congregations. They will be erected on the west side of Clifton Avenue, directly opposite Burnet Woods, on a lot having a frontage of seven hundred and fifty feet on the former thoroughfare and about twelve hundred feet deep.

The site is known as the Cook tract, and was sold to the Building Committee, composed of Sigmund Rheinstrom, Chairman; Isaac W. Bernheim, Sol Fox, J. Walter Freiberg, Louis W. Goldman, and Lipman Levy, Secretary, through Broker Jacob Shottenfels. These representatives of the institution provided for competitive plans which met with success. But five architects, all residents of Cincinnati, were invited to compete, and those of A. Lincoln Fechheimer, associated with Harry Hake, were decided to be the best. His sketches have just been returned from Atlanta, Georgia, where the organization recently held its annual meeting, and at which the plans were exhibited. One of the features of the session was the announcement of Isaac W. Bernheim, one of the Building Committee, who lives in Louisville, Kentucky, that he would pay the cost of building the library. This practically amounts to a donation of $50,000.

The character of the ground divides the site into two nearly equal parts, that facing the avenue being in the nature of a plateau, while the other is hilly, in some places dropping down one hundred feet below the level of the plateau. The buildings will be erected on the plateau, while the hilly grounds will be retained for recreation purposes. According to the accepted design, the approach to the plateau is by means of an imposing flight of stairs and ramps. Facing the avenue is the Administration Building, and to the right the library, while to the left is the chapel. These structures will cost about $250,000. It is intended to erect these immediately, and, consequently, when finished, they will represent a complete whole, and not necessarily dependent upon future buildings for the completion and beauty of the scheme as seen from the main entrance. Two future buildings will be erected toward the rear of the Administration Building, and are intended to form a quadrangle.

These buildings, both as regards interior and exterior, follow the famous English universities in their character, and it is believed this will give a serious and scholastic character to the whole scheme. The exterior will be of red brick, with stone trimmings, thus relieving the somber tone which would otherwise prevail.

The Administration Building will contain the President's offices, three boardrooms, and twelve classrooms, each seating from ten to twenty-five students. There will also be an auditorium, capable of seating two hundred people, which can also be used as a chapel. The library will have a general reading room approximating forty square feet. Three small reading rooms and the librarian's office will open from this general reading room. The stack rooms are planned to shelve fifty thousand volumes, and are capable of future extension. The chapel is designed to seat five hundred people.

[*THE COURIER-JOURNAL*, LOUISVILLE,
FEBRUARY 1, 1910.]

TRUSTEES FOR A COMMISSION

VOTE TO LEGISLATE THEMSELVES OUT OF OFFICE—SCHOOL BOARD COMMITTEE WILL GO TO FRANKFORT—STATUE OF LINCOLN FOR NEW MALE HIGH SCHOOL— GIFT OF UNKNOWN CITIZEN

The School Trustees joined the movement last night that has for its purpose the abolishment of the School Board through the agency of a bill before the Legislature providing for a commission asking that the measure be passed. The resolutions were offered by Dr. I. N. Bloom and seconded by Pink Varble and Dr. J. Hunter Peake. The trustees present—there were eleven—all seemed overjoyed at the opportunity to assist in legislating themselves out of office.

The resolutions provided that a committee of five be appointed by President R. J. Gough, to include himself, to go to Frankfort on the day the bill is reported out of committee to lend their efforts in hastening the vote that is to make it a law. President Gough appointed Trustees Bloom, Varble, Edelen, Rietze, and Gough as the committee. Secretary Charles C. Martin is to be a member of the body, as is also Norton Goldsmith, the Board's new attorney. Mr. Goldsmith was provided for under a separate resolution introduced by Dr. J. Hunter Peake. A resolution offered by Mr. Varble requested that Mayor W. O. Head, who is known to be heartily in favor of the measure's passage, join the School Board officials when they make their trip to the State's Capital.

The adoption of these resolutions was the only business transacted last night. Just before adjournment Mr. Goldsmith made memorable his first night as the Board's attorney by informing the members that an unnamed philanthropically inclined citizen of Louisville desired permission to present the Male High School with a statue of Abraham Lincoln. The statue is to be carved by one of the country's most famous sculptors and will be as imposing when completed as the Jefferson monument in front of the courthouse, which was the gift of the Bernheim brothers.

"Thoughts that were the seeds of action."

—EMERSON

GUIDING MAXIMS

Son, hear the instructions of thy father, and forsake not the law of thy mother.

Honesty is the best policy.

Do not buy what you do not want—it is dear at any price.

Credit is a looking-glass—easily broken.

Remember always that labor is one of the conditions of our existence.

Never bid another do what you cannot do yourself.

Never think any matter so trifling as not to deserve notice.

One today is worth two tomorrows.

Without economy very few would be rich: with it, none need be poor.

If you waste an hour or two every day, and a day or two every now and then, you will soon run out of time.

Either a man must be content with poverty or else be willing to deny himself some luxuries, and save to lay the basis of future independence.

The rich men of today were the sons of poor men forty years ago. Habits of saving made them so.

Build friendship on trade—don't build trade on friendship.

THE CLOSING
CHAPTERS
OF A BUSY LIFE

—————— ISAAC WOLFE BERNHEIM ——————

Previously Published by
WELCH-HAFFNER PRINTING CO.
DENVER, COLORADO, U.S.A.
DECEMBER 1929

CONTENTS

FOREWORD 139

SCHMIEHEIM 141

BERLIN AND HOME 157

ADDRESS DELIVERED BEFORE THE CONFERENCE OF
THE WORLD UNION FOR PROGRESSIVE JUDAISM . . 159

A MEMORIAL OF LOVE 165

ADDRESS DELIVERED AT THE DEDICATION OF THE
CAVE HILL MONUMENT 169

IN HONOR OF KENTUCKY 173

MY EIGHTIETH BIRTHDAY 179

MY DREAM 187

THE REFORM CHURCH OF AMERICAN ISRAELITES . 191

ISAAC WOLFE BERNHEIM: A PERSONAL STUDY 203

PRINTING presses the world over are running with ever-increasing speed to reproduce stories covering every phase of human endeavor, that man has to tell. They are also used by men in all walks of life to relate events that are, presumably, their own experiences. I am publishing this volume, not as a contribution to the literature of the day, but merely as an account of some of my activities, and primarily for my family and friends.

My life has not been spectacular, there have been no amazing adventures. It has been an ordinary life interspersed with light and shadow, happiness and depression. It has been uneventful, but always interesting.

In no sense is this book a biography, for my own history and that of my forebears was published in 1910 in a volume entitled "The Bernheim Family." However, I trust I may be pardoned for a personal pride, as today, in my retirement, I review the closing chapters of a busy life.

As a poor immigrant youth from Germany, where I was born, I arrived in New York. I have worked hard, and time was never checked by me in my career. I have carried a pack selling Yankee notions, and by toil I eventually created a large and prosperous business. I accumulated sufficient wealth to carry out the dreams of my youth, to pay my thanks in gifts or benefactions to my native town, the country of my adoption and to the State and City in which I gained commercial success, and I have done my duty to God, and have provided for my descendants.

I have established a Foundation which I feel confident will be of great benefit to the people in coming years in making their pathways brighter, and broadening their minds to the glory of Nature and Art.

I love labor, and, thank God, I am still able to perform it although I was eighty-one years old November fourth, nineteen hundred and twenty-nine. I trust that I shall retain strength, mental and physical, to continue to do the things from which the people in the years to come, as well as the present, shall find amidst pleasant surroundings wholesome lessons which will contribute to their happiness.

ISAAC WOLFE BERNHEIM
DENVER, 1929

I

SCHMIEHEIM

"Our home is home, be it ever so homely."

— CHARLES DIBDIN

THE call of childhood's home ever rings in the heart of a man. He may wander far from it, age may come with wealth or failure, but there still remains this remembrance and love of the place of his childhood.

A man may lose interest in those men and women with whom he has had close business relations, or he may even forget them, and if recalled to memory at all, he merely wonders if they be living or dead. In his tense business life the past may fade, but he ever retains a vivid memory of his boyhood with all its associations, scenes and personalities.

The call comes time and again to return, and to find, if possible, the companions of youth. His heart warms at the thought. Being of an intense disposition, perhaps this call is stronger in my heart than in that of the average man. I wandered far from Schmieheim, the village in Baden, Germany, where I was born November 4, 1848, and where my early boyhood was spent. I came to the United States in 1867, and landed, an immigrant, in Castle Garden with only four dollars of American money. I have had my struggles and my heartaches, my pleasures and my sorrows, and I have succeeded beyond the average emigrant youth—and I have heard and have responded to this call back to the scenes of my childhood.

This call came to me one morning, quite unexpectedly, but compellingly, and I answered, although a few moments before such a response was the farthest from my thoughts. In the fall of 1927, as was my custom, I was spending three or four weeks in New York. At that time I was a special partner in a Wall Street firm. I enjoyed the unrestricted run of its offices, and the privilege of hanging my coat and hat on my own peg in the inner closet. The entire office force knew me as the "Old Man."

It was one of those bracingly brilliant mornings which make New York in the fall one of the most delightful places on earth, when I left my hotel and walked briskly over to Fifth Avenue. Here the crowds checked my pace, and I was forced to stroll leisurely down to Twenty- first Street from where the elevated railroad took me to Rector Street, nearby my office.

It was my wont to glance over the morning papers on my way downtown. It may have been an interesting news item, it may have been an accident—perhaps destiny, but on this particular morning I inadvertently passed Rector Street and found myself at Battery Park. This compelled me to retrace my steps up Broadway to Rector Street.

THE VILLAGE OF SCHMIEHEIM

Have you ever walked up Broadway from the Battery? If so you may have been impressed by the many steamship offices. There is a continual movement of people in and out of them. Small groups of native and foreign-born citizens of all types around these offices interested me. Each told its story.

I lingered in front of the North German Lloyd Agency. Its flag floated gaily and gracefully in the breeze. I recognized it, of course, for under it I had crossed the Atlantic several times, in fact, one of its ships, the old *Hansa*, landed me in New York in 1867.

I stood there for a moment. The picture of its modern steamships displayed in the window attracted my attention. I had passed these

DURING MY LAST VISIT, 1928

offices hundreds of times before. They had meant no more to me than the many skyscrapers in the neighborhood, but on this particular morning a strange and unaccountable longing came over me to visit the scenes of my early life. It could not be called homesickness. I had lived in this blessed land for more than sixty years. In it centers everything that is dear to me. My family and all my material interests are here. I had taken root deep in the soil, and so had my children and grandchildren. By no stretch of the imagination could this longing be attributed to homesickness. I knew it as the call in my heart back to my boyhood home.

I stood there in reflection. I wanted to know how the little town in Germany looked. I was there last in 1912. How does it appear now? Would it be foolhardy for one of my advanced years to cross the ocean? Would the trip be worth the risk? These and many other questions arose in my mind, but the call overcame my misgivings. I stepped into the agency, and within thirty minutes I had contracted for a passage going and returning for myself, my wife and my secretary. I chose June as the month for sailing as business engagements would hold me at home until that time.

Schmieheim! The very name and the arranging for the journey awakened in me a host of memories.

Schmieheim, the little town where I was born, is in Baden, that part of Germany in the valley of the Rhine, made famous by its spas, and by the beauty of its scenery. It lies almost halfway between Baden Baden and Freiburg. Away from the main traveled road, and four miles distant from the nearest railway, it is a quaint village. Through it meanders the Unstrut, an insignificant and lazy creek. Its name does not appear on any of the German topographical maps, which may be construed as another confirmation of the old truth that often in the most inaccessible places there grow beautiful flowers. Far be it from me to make extravagant claims for Schmieheim, but in my boyhood days it occupied a position of outstanding importance.

In that far-off day it was a community of about twelve hundred inhabitants, and Israelites outnumbered Gentiles two to one. The business of the town was in their hands, much of the trade of the countryside for miles and miles around was controlled by them either as dealers, brokers, or as middlemen. It was a democratic community. There were but few well-to-do-among them, but there was contentment, and a wholesome state of economic sufficiency. Absolute poverty was unknown.

Evidence of a desire to reach out for the higher and better things of life was not entirely lacking. A rabbi lived there to look after the spiritual wants of the people. A reading club with a limited membership existed, as also did a singing society. Business was diversified and subdivided to a degree bordering on the ridiculous. The "Obrigkeit," that bureaucratic German regime, regulated every human activity down to the night watchman who patrolled the town with his lantern, and called each passing hour. Passports were required when visiting nearby towns. They were issued in the name of the bearer, with every detail noted, down to the color of the hair. A separate heading mentioned the line of business or trade the bearer was permitted to follow. When the "Obrigkeit" extended the privilege of dealing in shoestrings, or in horses, or in cattle, or in old iron and rags, or to have a tailor or shoemaker's shop the owner of the passport was, under the law, confined in his operations to that particular trade.

Educational facilities were meager, and limited to a single public school with one teacher. A grade school in the nearby county seat, Ettenheim, offered opportunity for a higher education. I walked there for three years, winter and summer, sans overcoat and underclothes, a distance of three miles. My schooling was finished in my thirteenth year.

All this relates to Schmieheim prior to 1861. The Schmieheim following the latter part of 1861, the time of the proclamation of the emancipation of the Jews in Baden, is an entirely different story. Schmieheim suffered retrogression, loss of prestige and shrinkage in population. Briefly, what for all of the Jews in the then Grand Duchy of Baden spelled a new epoch of liberty and justice, equality before the law and the possession of full civil rights, denoted for the village decay and ruin.

The fossilized, inhuman and autocratic laws which had hedged in that unhappy people, robbed them of manhood and treated them as outcasts and near slaves, disappeared as mist before the warming rays of a brilliant sun. Under the old order a Jew paid taxes, but was denied the right of suffrage, he was drafted into the military service but could not advance beyond the rank of corporal. Refused the right of domicile in nearly all of the towns of the country of his birth, he was the football of every bully, and at the mercy of every designing scoundrel in and out of office. Courts were open to the Jew, but Justice was non-existent. Disputes had to be settled by the local rabbi or by arbitration.

A new era dawned for those downtrodden people in the emancipation proclamation. The new law conferred upon them the right of suffrage and the privilege of holding office. Their movements were no longer restricted by the police or by the "Obrigkeit." They were free to follow any legitimate business of their own choosing in every city, town or village in the Grand Duchy of Baden.

The pent-up energy, ambition and enterprise, the inborn urge to better one's condition and to secure a wider sphere of activity all culminated in a mass emigration from that friendly town, and thus it was quickly emptied of the best part of its most desirable element. Real estate values dropped rapidly. The rabbi was transferred, the singing society ceased to sing and the reading club ceased to read. No one remained to tell of the old glory except the aged, the poor and the decrepit.

Our family was one of the first to leave Schmieheim, the town which had offered us, and many generations of Bernheims, the protection and comfort of a home. We settled in Freiburg, where, soon after our arrival, I was put to work as an apprentice in a linen store. I served three years without pay to learn the rudiments of German commerce. My employer was a strict disciplinarian. Punctuality in the performance of every duty was rigidly insisted upon. These traits became deeply ingrained in me, and although I chafed against his iron rule, as any natural, healthy boy would have done, in after years I recognized the value of the training I had received in that little store.

At the end of the second year of my apprenticeship I was placed in charge of the bookkeeping department, and so thorough and painstaking was my employer as my teacher, that in the third year I was competent to become bookkeeper for a local retail clothier during Sundays and in my spare hours. As compensation for this I received a ready-made suit of clothes for a year of work.

II

"The world is a great book of which they that never stir from home, read only a page"

ST. AUGUSTINE

SOON after midnight, June 9, 1928, following a hearty Godspeed from our children, relatives and friends, our cabin filled with flowers, Mrs. Bernheim and I, accompanied by Mr. Paul, my secretary, sailed on the S.S. *Columbus* from New York for Germany. From the moment of departure the weather was ideal, and all elements combined to make the voyage a delightful one.

As the steamer drew slowly to her anchorage at Bremerhaven, however, the air was cold, and a driving rain beat upon us as we were transferred from the tender to the quay. The tedious disembarkation was extremely trying to our nerves for we were anxious to put foot once more on solid ground. Nevertheless, tired though we were by the long waiting and the fatigue incident to the irritating landing formalities and custom procedure, all unpleasant feelings were dissipated immediately we had begun our journey to Bremen.

Once settled comfortably on the cushions of a spacious "Erste Klasse" we relaxed. As the boat special drew out of the long train-sheds, and we looked about us, we could not but feel that had we never visited Germany before, but had been transported blindfolded and then released in the train compartment alone, there would have been no difficulty in recognizing the countryside as Germany. The orderly arrangement of the dockside buildings, the neat streets, even the railroad sidings, the roadbed carefully ballasted and scrupulously free from weeds, spoke of the characteristics of the German people, system and cleanliness.

Even in the short ride from Bremerhaven to Bremen there was sufficient to bring back the sensation of being on my old home soil, and a warm feeling of kinship for the workmen and women in the streets below glowed in my heart.

We had taken the precaution to make reservations from the steamer for accommodations at Hillmans Hotel, in Bremen, for a rest of a few days before proceeding to Baden Baden. In a short time our land legs were regained, and amidst the comfort of the beautifully appointed hotel we enjoyed real German hospitality.

The usual quiet and customary reserve of the hotel was broken by a slight diversion, for Captain Hoehenfeld, Lieutenant Koehne and Major Fitzmaurice, the two German airmen, who, with their Irish companion, had returned on the *Columbus* after their successful flight across the Atlantic ocean, were guests of the hotel. All day, delegations, admiring countrymen, and the merely curious, thronged the reception rooms, and surged around the entrance like waves dashing over rocks at the seashore. The enthusiasm of the Bremeners, as evidenced by the fervor of the "Hoch Hochs," increased from hour to hour, and only the arrival of the mounted police who formed a cordon of automobiles around the hotel, prevented the crowd from taking Hillmans by storm.

We spent two or three days very pleasantly in Bremen enjoying the quaintness of the old town, and then boarded the day train for

Baden Baden. It is a ten-hour journey by express, and as the beautiful country rolled by we were continually enchanted and entertained by the varying types of people seen, and the many places of interest passed through. Our trip was broken by a short wait at Frankfurt where we changed to the Basle express, and soon we were alighting at the little town of Oos whence a short branch line landed us in Baden Baden.

The Hotel Stephanie concierge was at the station to meet us, and without worrying about baggage or being annoyed by those details of travel that sometimes make the most experienced voyager wish he had stayed at home, we were quickly taken to our hotel where Herr Brenner, the proprietor, was awaiting us. All was in readiness for us, and once ensconced in a beautiful suite of rooms overlooking the Lichtentaler Allee, all thoughts of the long journey from New York disappeared, and the rippling of the little river Oos outside our balcony seemed alone sufficiently well worth the effort.

The next day, June 21st my wife celebrated her 68th birthday. Gifts from her daughters surreptitiously brought with me, a little surprise dinner, and letters and cablegrams from home gave her enjoyment on her anniversary. In the afternoon I took her on a short tour of the town and showed her many of the famous landmarks. As we drove up the gentle hills along winding roads, vistas of almost unimaginable beauty opened to our view. At every turn we came to realize that Baden Baden certainly lived up to its reputation. Always a favorite with European nobility, ever since their forefathers discovered the health-giving springs which abound, the town, like all German municipalities, is immaculately clean, and everywhere there are flowers. There are enough amusements for the vigorous and the pleasure-seeking tourist, and plenty of quiet for those who wish it.

We spent our days enjoying the shade of the beautiful walks, visiting the concert room in the new Kurhaus, or listening to the orchestra in the Garden. In the afternoon we could sit at one of the small tables under the gaily colored umbrellas and marvel at the intricacies of the tango. The groups of people, of every type and of most nationalities, enjoying their refreshments under the trees or on the terrace of the Kurhaus never failed to be of interest.

Baden Baden is one of the oldest watering places in Europe. Eighteen hundred years ago the Emperor Hadrian had built a bathhouse there, yet it possesses an immortal youth, and, cannot fail to impress even the most blase traveler as a place that for natural beauty has no rivals. There are dozens of hot springs. How fascinating it is to watch the water bubble out. The great Frederich Spring is the largest of them all, and here one may see the pretty flaxen-haired maids bringing their large pails to the spring to get the boiling water.

The town itself, nestling in the valley surrounded as it is by lute-shaped hills, each one with its ruined tower, a reminder of the Margraves is a delight. The winding hilly roads, the waterways that twist and turn in and out of the streets, the terraced walls, the gardens, the multitudinous baskets of hanging flowers add to the picturesqueness. As we walked along the narrow byways seeking shade from the July sun our interest was arrested frequently by works of art and other treasures reposing retiringly in the small shop windows. It is the sort of place that one dreams of existing only on a picture postcard.

But in a wider and more intimate sense, the section and vicinity of Baden Baden was to me my boyhood home. The Schwarzwald, its hillsides densely wooded with aromatic pines, the well-kept roads intersected by shady trails, the vineyards on the sunny slopes and the meadows and wheatfields in the valleys brought back memories of the long ago. Nature eternally beautiful, man the football of every whim of Destiny!

Thus, on my last visit in nineteen hundred and twelve I had seen the country at its best. Then contentment and prosperity pervaded all classes, today depression and a genteel poverty were visible on every corner. The sight depressed me greatly and robbed me at the beginning of the joy nearly always felt by the tourist who has traveled long distances to reach an anxiously longed-for goal.

III

MID SCENES of CHILDHOOD

"The whitewashed wall, the nicely sanded floor,
The varnish'd clock that click'd behind the door."

— GOLDSMITH

I HAD selected Baden Baden as our headquarters, for from there splendid automobile roads reached every community with which I was familiar, and which were closely associated with my boyhood, including Schmieheim. A ride of two hours by motor car would take me to all the communities I wished to visit. But it was to the village where I was born that I had crossed the ocean, responding to that call back to the home of my childhood.

I wonder if many men visiting their youthful homes have suffered the shock I had when I entered Schmieheim? The world war had taken its toll of people and left its grim mark on the village. The change to me was startling and sad. In place of the trim homes and neat streets, in place of the happy and contented citizens, I found streets uncleaned, houses neglected, many of them tenantless, with their shutters tightly closed, and the residents disheartened.

I had last visited my birthplace in 1912 — sixteen years before - but on entering, the village itself had so little altered that I had not the slightest difficulty in going directly to the house where I was born. The house, since my family left for Freiburg, had passed through many ownerships, and now was occupied by a good woman who maintained it in the scrupulous cleanliness of my boyhood.

As I stepped over the threshold upon invitation of the woman, what memories flashed through my mind! It was in this room and from that very beam in the ceiling that my mother hung the first coal oil lamp to be used in the village. I well remember the marvel of its brilliancy to our childish eyes, accustomed, as we were to candlelight. Every nook and every cranny had its memories for me.

While I was asking questions and recounting incidents of the long ago, news of my presence had spread and looking out of the window I saw a group of men and women assembled in the yard. They had come to welcome me, and I joined them. As I singled out the ones whom I had met on my previous visit, I was overjoyed that they could answer the many questions that I asked them. The fate of friends, — alas, the deaths — the condition of affairs, were queries that sprang to my lips. More and more as one told the tale, and others came forward to amplify and add their word, the more distressing it became to hear of the sad lot that had befallen so many. How many good and honest people through no fault of their own had been reduced to penury by the world war. Only the middle-aged and the very young were left. An entire generation of youth had disappeared, whilst the privations of the war years had been the death of the older residents, Few indeed remained who had reached their allotted three score years and ten.

Although Schmieheim was no longer the spruce, prosperous village it once had been, and despite the broken tiles of the roofs, patched houses with water-stained walls, the unpaved streets and generally dejected appearance, the interior of the homes of even the humblest spoke of care, diligence and economy, and cleanliness. Their poverty may have cut deep into their bodies, but their souls were untouched and there was no trace of that debasement which acute poverty so frequently brings in its train.

My first objective, after satisfying the curiosity of so many of the people, was to visit the Jewish cemetery. In this ancient graveyard, my father, my sisters, and my brothers who died in their childhood are in their last resting places. I stood on this hallowed ground, with bowed head. My father died January 9, 1856, in his forty-eighth year, leaving my sainted mother with four children of whom, I, the oldest, had just finished my seventh year,

The Jewish community, a mere remnant of that body of citizens who in former days were really the life and blood of the village, had dwindled away through lack of trade, and by emigration, until the congregation of the Synagogue numbered a bare thirty families. It had been sad enough to listen to the stories of their hardships as individuals, but what seemed to me even more distressing was that their collective spirit of hope and enterprise was broken. They expressed little faith in the future, and could see but faint light on the horizon.

It has always been my theory of life that the able-bodied, the young and the middle-aged can fend for themselves under even the most adverse circumstances. The giving of alms and undiscriminating charity which destroys the self respect of the recipient never appealed to me, but I could not help being touched by the plight of the young children, orphans, and the aged.

As I listened during my visits to all the stories of misfortune, saw the humble homes, and the lack of comforts, my mind turned to those of my co-religionists who would find it impossible to support themselves. I enquired how the children were taken care of, the manner of maintaining the orphans, the aged and the afflicted. I was told that previous to the last war there had always been sufficient funds to maintain a "Waisenverein," and there was also a Home for the Aged in the town of Gailingen. The years of the war, followed by the destruction of the Mark, had taken away all the resources of these two benevolent agencies, and left them poverty stricken, without the means to carry on. Throughout the village, as I walked about revisiting familiar scenes, and talking with the men and women, it became apparent to me that here was a body of my own people, still staunch to their faith, isolated from the world and slowly dying of inanition.

Public spirit, as understood by us in America, is almost an unknown quantity in Germany, as it is in fact throughout Europe. Do not understand me to say that philanthropists do not exist. They unquestionably do, but it must be conceded that according to our conception their standard is far below ours. The municipalities take the place of the European philanthropist. Parks, theatres, hospitals, schools, zoological gardens and all similar enterprises contributing to the intellectual, physical or artistic life of the people are supported entirely by a system of taxation.

The expression of my readiness to do something for the public good of Schmieheim was joyfully received by Jew and Gentile. My friend Dr. Kassewitz, of Freiburg, a lawyer of distinction and proven capacity, represented me in the negotiations with the Burgomaster of the local council. The town needed many things, but it was finally decided that a modern waterworks system would fill the most urgent need. My contribution enabled the village to secure a pure and ample supply of water.

Schmieheim possesses a landmark, the "Schloss" or Castle, an architectural abomination of no value, at one time the property of an impoverished noble family who disappeared from the scene some centuries ago. It is now owned by the municipality, but in my childhood days it served the dual place of a public school and residence of the Rabbi. I looked it over from cellar to garret, a mere shell, and a roost of bats and owls. The two acres surrounding it were a pasture for a few goats of poor people, but the two great sycamores, objects of adoration of my boyhood, still stood, silent witnesses to the departed glory of the vicinity.

The old castle and its environs attracted me, and I was impressed by its possibilities. The ground within its walls could be made into a park for the old and a playground for the children. The ruin could be converted into a social center for the villagers and an attraction for all the neighborhood. This would put a touch of modern life into the community. The idea appealed to me and might have been carried out had I not been informed by the "Obrigkeit" that in Germany ruins must remain ruins. The restoration, if undertaken, would depend on the permission of the Government. My time was too limited for such negotiations, and the plan was reluctantly abandoned.

The one other outstanding architectural feature of the village is the Lutheran Church. Its dedication occurred when I was a youngster, but I can remember what a big event that was for every man, woman and child in the community. The ceremony is vivid in my mind as if it had taken place but yesterday.

The Synagogue in my childhood appeared like a skyscraper to me, On one of my previous visits its rundown and neglected condition was called to my attention by the president of the Congregation. My brother and I had it renovated and repaired under the direction of a competent architect of Freiburg. It stands today the one building of the entire village unaffected by the air of decay and neglect of its surroundings.

As on former visits, and, again on the one of which I am writing, I strolled about the town. Every foot was familiar territory to me. Here was the home of one of my school friends, nearby, the homes of several of my aunts and uncles, and not far away the residence of my grandfather. There, still stands the old brewery where I had my first taste of beer, and which today is the only live industry in the village. Its product has a good reputation and is distributed by motor trucks to the neighboring towns.

There is a strong streak of sentiment in my nature. The memories of bygone days, the ever-present fact that there remained not one living person in the village with whom I played or knew in boyhood; that even many of those whom I had met on my visit in 1912, had moved away or died, that there was not one with whom I could talk and who could talk with me of the olden days, became exceedingly depressing. Truly it seemed to me that I had "lived to be, the last leaf on the tree," and it was with a sense of sadness that I left the town.

IV

"Giving is true having."

I HAVE written of some of my contributions to public welfare in Germany, contributions, I am glad to say, that have not only been appreciated, but which have been of material benefit to those whom I sought to aid. Truth compels me to admit that charity in its generally accepted sense never has been one of my strong points. Charity is often misplaced, and fails to accomplish the good anticipated by the donors.

For years it had been my custom to support on a modest scale two charitable institutions in the then Grand Duchy of Baden. I am referring to the "Landesverein zur Erziehung Israelitischer Waisen," or Orphan Society, and the "Friedrichsheim für Israelitsche Sieche und arme Greise," "The Old Folks Home for Israelites," at Gailingen. At the close of the World War, when hunger, deprivation and poverty stalked throughout Germany, the appeal for funds to continue their work became increasingly urgent, and my contributions correspondingly larger. During my recent visit I found on personal investigation that both institutions filled ably and creditably their spheres of usefulness.

I motored from Baden Baden to Bruchsal, which is the seat of the Directorate of the Orphan Society. There I had a conference with Herr Jacob Oppenheimer, a charitably minded businessman, in whose hands the affairs of the Waisenverein are placed. He told me that the care of the Jewish orphans and fatherless children was under the control of the "Society for the Care and Education of Orphans of the Jewish Faith in Baden." The system of maintenance adopted by them is modern, and compares favorably with those used in other progressive communities. The children, instead of being housed in an orphanage, are boarded with good families where they can have the benefit from wholesome home influence.

Their funds were almost depleted at the time of my visit, and as a result of my conference with Herr Oppenheimer I offered him a sufficient sum to materially increase its capacity. A recent report from the Director brought me the gratifying assurance that the number of orphans taken care of by the Society has measurably increased.

Gailingen is the seat of the "Old Folks Home for the Aged and Infirm." It is a small and unimportant town in the southeastern corner of Baden, near the Bodensee, and in the neighborhood of Ludwigshaven, the home of the German Zeppelin industry. To reach the town by motor from Baden Baden would require five hours. Lack of time and the prevailing high temperatures prevented a personal inspection of the institution.

Dr. Sigmund Kassewitz has served as its president for many years, and, as previously stated, he is a most estimable and trustworthy man, standing high in the community as a practicing attorney. At a meeting in Freiburg, and later at one in Baden Baden attended by a member of the Board, I convinced myself from submitted printed reports extending over a considerable number of years, that its activities covered every urgent need among my poor co-religionists, and that the affairs of the Old Folks Home were well managed and carried on ably and creditably. I donated the amount necessary to cover the cost of construction of a new wing, which has now been completed and which has doubled the capacity.

As the summer days passed Mrs. Bemheim and I spent delightful hours travelling the countryside to places of beauty and of interest, but ever was I drawn back to the little town of Schmieheim. I felt a need to linger among the men of the village, men whose lives, restricted and yet content in many ways, would have been my own if chance had not removed me to other spheres. There was a tenderness in the cool depths of the Synagogue, and when I visited it I was touched to see the gratitude of the congregation expressed on a tablet thanking my brother and me for making possible the repairs needed so badly when I was in Schmieheim in the year 1910.

V
BERLIN AND HOME

"Pleasure is the flower that fades, remembrance is the lasting perfume."

— BOUFFLERS

THE reader may possibly have wondered why when I had felt the call back to my childhood home in Germany in the fall of 1927, I had delayed my departure until June, 1928. Perhaps I should explain that whilst commercial engagements and other personal affairs demanded much of my time, and prevented an immediate answer to the summons in my heart, I was also an accredited delegate to the World Conference of Progressive Judaism in Berlin to be held August 18-21, of that year. I realized that even if I could have left at once, my age precluded two trips to Germany within so short a time.

The days spent in Baden Baden passed rapidly, and finally the time allotted for quiet and rest in that beautifol resort came to an end. After a short visit to Switzerland and a week spent in Paris, we arrived in Berlin on August 12.

Reform Judaism has always been close to my heart, and it was my earnest desire to bring to the conference some suggestions emphasizing the necessity for granting the Jewish Layman a voice in the Councils now largely controlled by the Rabbinate. I felt this was the urgent need of Judaism of today, if the reactionaries, who of recent years had proved a preponderating influence, were to be defeated.

The preliminary meetings were held on Saturday and Sunday, the speeches were made almost exclusively by rabbis, and were of a technical, or rather, theological nature. The living issues of Reform Judaism were seemingly neglected by them. The following Monday was reserved for the discussion of the papers read on the preceeding days, and at the morning session I was the first one called upon to speak.

As I mounted the platform and looked over the audience of my co-religionists, with the words of the rabbis and professional religionists ringing in my ears, I felt a great desire to deliver my message and arouse in my hearers an appreciation of the dangers with which Liberal Judaism was threatened. The reception I received was well nigh unbelievable. I had scarcely read the introductory ideas of my subject when it became painfully evident to me that the tenor of my remarks was not to the liking of my hearers, nor to the powers in control. They took quick opportunity to call me to order, and by a subterfuge prevented me from delivering the remainder of my message.

Their storm of protest rose hostilely against me, and as I listened to their cries of "Nein, Nein" when the Chair appealed to their sporting instincts to give me a further hearing, the word "Progressive" used in the title of the conference seemed to me somewhat inappropriate. The thoughts and sentiments expressed by a majority of the speakers at the various sessions may have been considered progressive in Eastern Europe or in Asia Minor, but could hardly be thought of as such when compared with the standards of liberalism reached in America.

Our German co-religionists evidently have not learned as yet that the man who in sincerity and knowledge criticizes or dissents from some well-established institution, idea, or cause, is as much entitled to that dissent as his fellow who defends what he condemns. It is a hard lesson for public opinion in a democracy to learn. There were, however, a few bright lights to relieve the gloom, chief of whom was Rabbi Doctor Lehman, of Berlin; but taken as a whole there appeared to be a sense of frustration and recession among these European members of my religion.

The weather, which throughout the entire time we spent in Germany had been exemplary, continued to be delightful. This enabled us to enjoy the remainder of our stay in Berlin to the fullest.

On the twenty-fifth of August, once more on board the friendly *Columbus*, we sailed for home. Another perfect sea trip, the ocean as calm as a mill pond, and we were in New York. After the usual annoying formalities with the Customs, we were glad to put foot on land, saying, "Home once more, back in God's own country after all the best place to be." My son, Palmer, and his wife were at the pier to meet us, and quickly escorted us to our hotel, whence after a few days rest we returned to our summer home in Denver.

ADDRESS
Delivered before the Conference of
THE WORLD UNION FOR PROGRESSIVE JUDAISM
August 18-21, 1928, Berlin

I DO not possess the academic discipline which some of you enjoy, neither am I learned in the law, nor informed accurately in the historic development of our faith, but as a layman and humble worker I have in a rather active life observed many phases of our religious progress. I owe my inspiration to my two sainted teachers in Israel, Dr. Adolph Moses, of Louisville, Ky., and Dr. Isaac M. Wise of Cincinnati, Ohio, the incomparable leaders of American Reform Israel. Their personalities and teachings formed me, and to this day, although both of them have been gathered to their fathers, their spirit still dominates my thinking and my being.

If I were to estimate the value of their contribution to our thought succinctly, I would say that both of them stressed the universality of the religion of Israel. Under the sway of social, economic and political influences of their day, they came to the conclusion that the universal element in our religion must be recalled from the mass of customs, ceremonials and mediaeval influences which threatened many a time wholly to submerge the finest product of its genius. This product was, undoubtedly, the prophetic element in our religion. And by prophetic, I do not, of course, intend to convey the notion of prediction, but rather the idea of consecration under the hand of God to the fundamental principles of Israel's faith.

The religion of Israel, as I have been taught, was primarily a practical faith, an attempt to adjust the present to certain imperishable ideals of justice, mercy and humble trust in Divine Providence. There was, of course, needed, as always there will be, organization, authority, special days set aside for religious meditation, certain unique ways of expressing its thought, all of which have been incorporated in our ritual and in our life.

I have no quarrel with any of these as long as they express the truth, as interpreted by farseeing and religious men who live in the present and have an eye to the future. I am not pleading for a meaningless universalism, but I am emphasizing the need for always keeping in the foreground the moral and spiritual purpose of our life. This has been expressed to a measurable degree in the Reform Movement of American Israelites. I am aware that even in this branch there has not been uniformity. Nor is that desirable. Some of us are more attached to ancient ways than are others. Some of us are living in an environment in which the past has more direct influence upon us than it has in other sections of the world. But, we are all united in this one, definite idea: "Our faith must cease to be a tribal religion." This must be accepted, at least in its underlying principle, by any people who wish to subject themselves to its beneficent sway.

A number of conclusions issue from this thesis, chief of these is the doctrine that we are not a nation and that we are determined not to isolate ourselves in Palestine. We are utterly opposed and will never willingly or otherwise subscribe to Israel's identification with a national policy or culture, nor will we recognize in any form a flag or national hymn other than the ones in the land in which we live. We shall never allow any man or set of men to lead us astray by sentimental and transient humanitarian appeals, to endorse a movement like Political Zionism, which gives the lie to all the preachings of our Prophets and to historical movements within the last two thousand years.

A limited number of our leaders, for one reason or another, have been tempted to compromise with this. It is high time to let the world know that we Liberal Reform Israelites insist that our faith is not merely one of the by-products of our people, but that it is the heart, the nucleus and the reason for our existence now and forever. It appears to me that this international organization of our liberal brethren is obligated once more to take this definite stand. On this we can all unite, and with this inscribed on our banner, we can move forward.

Let me not be misunderstood as one who has no sympathy with those of our co-religionists who can find no other refuge but in Palestine. We are eager and willing to lend our aid to any colonization movement which has for its aim their settlement in Palestine. We cherish the historic associations that bind us to that classic land. We revere the idealistic motives that have brought many of our people there. But we are unalterably opposed, let it be said again, to the institution of a Judaic Political State, in this or any other land.

With the theological reconstruction of the faith of Israel on a liberal basis, I have at present, no concern. As a layman I am primarily interested in the practical issues. And, the purpose of my coming here is to place before you the formulation of a great need. Reform or Liberal Israel received its impetus from a layman, Israel Jacobson, and it may be remembered with profit that another layman, Moses Mendlessohn, prepared the way for its introduction into our larger life. But, as frequently happens, leadership in this has gotten into the hands of professionals, namely, the Rabbinate. This is not said in derogation of our Rabbis, practically all of whom have been earnest, devoted men. But I say this in chastisement of our laity, who have allowed themselves to become merely passive listeners and followers. No movement can prosper unless it has backing, and the cooperation of the great mass, and we laymen have been remiss in that we have yielded to those men that active participation which a successful movement demands.

My particular suggestion is that now is the time to inaugurate a lay organization of our liberal Reform Co-religionists the world over, which will enthusiastically further our cause. The details of its organization I leave to this assembly.

It is not to be understood in any sense as an opposition party, nor as a desire to capture leadership, but in all humility to demonstrate that thousands upon thousands of Israelites have caught the spirit of our liberal thought and wish to enroll themselves in this high and noble cause.

This proposed organization of laymen is, after all, not a new and untried thing. In America we already have a number of federations of Men's Clubs, which despite their youth, have accomplished some very significant things. They have, first of all, made the layman feel that he is an integral part of the working consciousness of Israel. He participates in congregational affairs, plans for the furtherance of its aims, and assumes its religious obligations and responsibilities. Practically it has resulted in increased devotion to the Synagogue, in more frequent and devout attendance upon its services, and a wholesome identification with everything that is best in our religious organization. It has created and maintained scholarships, both in our Theological Seminaries and in other institutions of learning. The organization has been the right hand of the rabbi, and I doubt not in the coming years will further multiply its usefulness. What is needed now is an extension of this principle to the end that a worldwide Lay Organization be effected. Its first duties, especially in those lands in which the reform spirit has not yet achieved organization, will be to found movements expressive of our liberal ideas. Surely, in many places on the European Continent there must be numerous men and women who are either merely nominally members of the existing Orthodox or Conservative Congregations, or they are entirely unaffiliated with a religious group. Their excuse has always been that they are not in sympathy with orthodoxy as it is presented to them, but they would ally themselves with a movement that was more authentically expressive of their own liberal views.

If we leave this entirely to the rabbis, not only will the progress of our cause be delayed but the movement itself may come under suspicion. The rabbis unaided cannot effect this change. We must give them an instrument whereby they may come to these unaffiliated, with the assurance that there is a great tide of opinion and belief sweeping in their direction. Perhaps one of the justifiable accusations leveled at our Reform Movement is this passivity of ours. The orthodox have again and again indulged themselves in their little jest that we call ourselves "par excellence" the missionary faith, but that we do no missionary work even among our own who need it most. If we have the courage of our convictions we should spread the good tidings among all our people who have grown dissatisfied with what seems to them dead formalism and an inert faith. The mechanism for this should be easily established. We need a thorough realization of its necessity by those of us who are here, the vanguard of the Liberal Movement.

This International Laymen's League, if organized, ought to provide a link between the fine body of teaching bequeathed to us by our rabbis and the great masses of laymen and women who are eager to receive it. I have heard, over and over again, statements to the effect that we must acquaint our people with the vast resources of our great literature, that we must establish on a firmer footing, our religious education, that we must teach our people its truths and to apply them to their daily life. Let this league be the practical instrument for the work.

Then, too, it is high time to put responsibility where it belongs. If there is any truth established by modern teachers, it is this, that the people cannot learn except through responsibility. The rabbis have long enough shouldered the burden. It is time to put a stop to the mockery of a religious life or ritual expressed largely through the rabbis. We laymen should be glad to assume this responsibility. One of the reasons for the cynicism current in our ranks has been that religious duties have not been brought home to the laity with sufficient force. No one can be a cynic when actively engaged in any humanitarian or religious task. Our young men and our young women, to whom the Synagogue has been a mausoleum, visited only in a rare mood of pious devotion to the past, will get a new view of our faith and our ideals. They will realize that ours is a religion of deed and aspiration, and that it is the duty of all born into the faith to carry on this noblest of all work.

Let us not also forget that ours is a democratic faith. Before the days of the high tide of industrialism, Israel, its teachings and its practices, was in the possession of all the people. As a consequence of the intense specialization of our day, it has been remanded largely to our rabbis. We must again capture this democratic mood. I have the profoundest conviction that when our progressive faith is popularized and democratized, there will be new access of energy streaming into our ranks. Its beauties will be made clear to them, and they will, like the Children of Israel at the foot of Mt. Sinai, again exclaim, "We have heard and we will do."

The future does not seem dark to me. In Christian circles there is a Youth Movement, in which there has been a revaluation of current doctrines and dogmas. As far as I can see, these young people are earnest and sincere. They insist upon creating and assuming the responsibility for their own faith. Why can we not have a similar piece of work among our own youth? We have at least this advantage, that ours is a rational religion, that we are not afraid to subject its tenets to the most careful scientific scrutiny, that our code of ethics has been adopted by the civilized world as the most respectable and fundamental of all moral principles. But, there must be an end to Defeatism, of which the Political Zionist is the foremost sponsor.

We do not believe that national chauvinism will continue to grow. We do not believe that prejudice against us will constantly increase. We do not believe that history will move backward, and that Israelites will find peace only in their exclusive environment. We must be willing to stake our cause on this hope which our own prophets have so comprehensively expressed. Our God is the God of all nations, our cause is the cause of all humanity, our faith may be accepted by all individuals who have found their way out of the morass of superstition and formalism into the broad plains and up the steep mountain sides of universalism.

A MEMORIAL OF LOVE

*"Let me dream, that love goes
with us to the shores unknown."*

— FELICIA HEMANS

IN the twilight of life man realizes that the shadows are growing deeper. It is a period that cannot be sensed by those younger than himself. The passing day but signifies the end of another swing of the pendulum whose swift and unrelenting tempo marks the flight of time, and draws him nearer, ever nearer, to the door of the Unknown.

I am remindful that birthdays are but stepping-stones to the inevitable end, but I believe that on the eve of my seventy-eighth birthday this realization came to me more forcibly than ever before, or since. As the natal day approached I made arrangements for its observance, for such an anniversary should be an occasion for memories, a time to be surrounded by one's own children, grandchildren and intimate friends, and to visit long familiar scenes.

November 4, 1926, marked my arrival at my seventy-eighth milestone. I journeyed to Cincinnati to pass the day quietly, for the preceding years had been full of sorrow for me, and there I could be with my family. I planned, also, at this time to dedicate a memorial to my wife.

On the morning of the following day — November 5th, — my family and I traveled in a private car over the Louisville and Nashville Railway from Cincinnati to Louisville to hold in Cave Hill Cemetery the ceremony long planned by me, the unveiling of the statue "Let There Be Light" which I had erected above my wife's last resting place.

The day was not propitious. The Indian Summer, for which Kentucky is famous, that year had been early, and of but short duration. It had given place to cold, damp and dreary weather. The rain which had threatened from early morning had not fallen, but the moisture in the air was forming a slight drizzle which caused the stripped and leafless trees to drip dampness from bole and branch.

What my thoughts were as I stood there, alone, on the ground hallowed by memories of my loved companion, and some day to receive my own earthly remains, none will ever know. For a few moments I faltered, but whatever emotions surged within me, I was able to suppress. I summoned all my willpower, and standing erect, faced my descendants. I spoke slowly as I delivered my dedicatory address, a tribute to my wife, and to my sons and brother who had gone into the Beyond. Then I spoke a few frank words to those around me, speaking from the heart to my remaining children.

As I ceased, the veil enshrouding the statue, released by my granddaughter, Miss Jane Rauh, floated down to reveal the upraised arms of the beautiful figure, inspiringly patient, awaiting through the ages past and to come the fruition of the Creator's edict, "Let There Be Light." With the reading of a few Psalms selected for their beauty and familiarity, the ceremony ended.

Then the shadows seemed to deepen around me, the day more gloomy and the wind more mournful through the trees. The floodgates of memory opened and the days that were gone never to return poured through my brain and into my heart with a weight that seemed more than I could bear. My family and friends appreciated my feelings. Sadly and compassionately they gazed upon me as I leaned against the base of the memorial to her who had fought by my side the struggles and shared the joys. Then they quietly stepped away, entered their cars and left me, as I longed to be — alone.

"LET THERE BE LIGHT,"
BY GEORGE GRAY BERNARD

ADDRESS
Delivered at the Dedication of the
CAVE HILL MONUMENT
November 5, 1926

IN the early hours of December 9, 1922, nearly four years ago, a blow fell from which I have to this day but faintly recovered. My good, unforgettable wife, your dear mother and grandmother, was called away in her sixty-eighth year, after a happy union extending over forty-eight years.

Less than a year thereafter, on November 14, 1923, my oldest son, Lee, was called in his forty-ninth year. His was a rugged nature. A Spartan in morality, a humanitarian of high ideals which would have found their fullest fruition had destiny accorded him a greater number of years.

On July 27, 1925, my brother, Bernard, who had worked alongside of me from boyhood on, passed away in his seventy-fifth year.

On May 8, 1926, I suffered the loss by death of my second oldest son, Morris, in the prime of his manhood, a good father, a model citizen, his life ended just as his work began to show the results he had so single mindedly and steadily labored for.

Sorrow, as storms bring down the clouds to earth, happily prove the instruments of cleansing and consolation. In the days of deep distress and severe heartaches I realized most gratefully that Fate had not been unkind to me, but that I had received favors above my deserts. I had been reasonably successful in my occupation. Honors were never sought nor popularity courted, yet I received a larger share than commonly comes into the life of an emigrant boy who seeks these shores with good intentions, but penniless.

It was a pleasure to accumulate wealth, but it gave me greater pleasure to share it, in part, in the community in which I lived, in the state which afforded me protection, in the nation whose citizenship I value as priceless, no less than in causes affecting my co-religionists, the stepchildren of the Ages.

I would be immodest were I to mention the causes, which at one time or another, received the benefit of my assistance. It was my privilege to provide liberally for my children and to enjoy the prospective satisfaction of rendering a similar service to the generation which is to follow them. To thus round out one's activity, in so far as it relates to one's earthly affairs, is indeed a privilege which comes to human beings only in isolated cases. To be singularly endowed with good health and to possess faculties unimpaired is a God-given distinction enjoyed by but few men at the age of seventy-eight. For this I am devoutly grateful to a kind Providence.

I have now arrived at the last stage of my work, the dedication of this monument marking the last resting place of your dear Mother. It is the handiwork of one of America's most renowned sculptors, nobly expressing his conception of God's command at the creation of the world, "Let There Be Light." It illustrates in strikingly beautiful form the hope and aspiration of all civilizations.

Light is the symbol of truth, it is the great corrective. A thousand wrongs and abuses that are grown in darkness disappear in the light of day. And thus, my dear ones let the light of reason, of tolerance, of fairness, and the virtues of good citizenship guide you, and you need never be ashamed to look squarely into the faces of your fellow men.

I see in my mind's eye, at no distant day, a thin line of mourners following the coffin containing my earthly remains, to rest in the spot now consecrated by her who for so many years was my companion, and who shared my cares, worries and tribulations, no less than the pleasures of my busy life. To both of us came the blessings of a life rich in all its phases. We were happiest and most contented by our fireside. We will sleep in death united beneath this sod amid these serenely beautiful surroundings, a piece of Kentucky which she and I have loved so well, and wherein we had spent our lives and lived most happily.

I look forward to the great adventure, which now cannot be far off, with awe, but not with apprehension. I shall be sorry to part with my children, grandchildren, home and friends, but always I have stood at the bow looking forward with hopeful anticipation of the life before me. When the time comes for my embarkation, I think I shall be standing at the bow, and still looking forward with eager curiosity to the new world to which the unknown voyage will bring me.

Nothing is indestructible in this world. Even bronze, the metal of the greatest durability, must yield to the natural life of the universe, but let me express the wish, that while this lovely figure points appealingly heavenward it may well serve its purpose of Hope which is the mainspring of human action, the passport to the soul's true and lasting happiness.

IN HONOR OF KENTUCKY

"The sun shines bright in
my old Kentucky home. . ."

— STEPHEN FOSTER

IN the course of an active business career I was frequently called to Washington, and on these occasions whenever I had the opportunity I would visit the public buildings and memorials. All my life an ardent admirer of sculpture, particularly of monumental art, I spent many hours in Statuary Hall where I enjoyed viewing the statues of those men deemed worthy by their States to represent them in the Hall of Fame.

Whilst walking under the rotunda of that historic building, a sense of humiliation overcame me to find that my own State — Kentucky — where I had lived for more than sixty years, and which I held in deep affection, was as yet unrepresented here although she had given many great and eminent men to America. The absence of statues of Kentuckians in the National Hall of Fame seemed to me the more regrettable as the greater number of the States had filled their allotted places. This implied a lack of pride on part of Kentucky citizens.

On my return to Louisville after one of my visits to Washington I decided to offer to the State of Kentucky the gift of bronze statues to represent two of Kentucky's most eminent citizens in positions of honor alongside those of the other States. At the next session of the Kentucky Legislature, Hon. Leon P. Lewis, one of the representatives from the Louisville district, made the formal offer of the gift before the assembled house on my behalf, and on March 16, 1926, the House of Representatives, with the Senate concurring, passed a resolution accepting my gift, and as an expression of its gratitude ordered that a copy of the resolution should be sent to me.

A commission consisting of the President of the University of

Kentucky, the President of Berea College and the President of the University of Louisville was appointed and they proceeded promptly to ascertain through popular vote of the school children of the State which of the eminent men of Kentucky were to have the honor of representing their State. The children, conferring with their parents, were in this way able to reflect the opinion of the majority of the people in the State. As might have been predicted, Abraham Lincoln and Henry Clay were the first favorites. The third ranking highest was Doctor Ephraim McDowell, the famous surgeon. When the result of the voting was considered by the Commission, on April 22, 1927, in the Kentucky Hotel, Louisville, Ky., and in conjunction with the Art Commission in Washington, it was agreed that because of the numerous statues of Lincoln already erected in the Capitol it would be more appropriate to select Henry Clay and Ephraim McDowell.

EPHRAIM MCDOWELL
STATUARY HALL — NATIONAL CAPITOL
WASHINGTON, D.C.

As soon as I was advised of the decision of the Statue Commission

HENRY CLAY
STATUARY HALL — NATIONAL CAPITOL
WASHINGTON, D.C.

I sought for a sculptor of outstanding ability and prominence to execute the work. After extensive investigation and correspondence with many of the great artists of America, I finally selected Charles Henry Niehaus as the one whose work over many years had fitted him best for the task.

Mr. Niehaus, immediately the preliminary details were settled, commenced his work with enthusiasm. To obtain materials, portraits, sketches, masks, etc., of Henry Clay was an easy matter, for the great Pacificator had frequently been the subject of the painter's brush and the sculptor's chisel. The famous surgeon, on the other hand, apart from the local medical societies, and the place of his birth, had been comparatively neglected, and it became necessary for Mr. Niehaus to do considerable searching before he was able to secure sufficiently reliable representations of Doctor McDowell to enable him to model the figures.

By the spring of 1929 Mr. Niehaus had finished the statues to his satisfaction, and all was ready for their erection in Statuary Hall and their unveiling. The exercises were arranged for two-thirty in the afternoon of March 3, 1929. The Hon. H. H. Kincheloe, representative from Kentucky, kindly undertook the work of arranging the program, and secured the speakers necessary to make the function one of distinction.

The day was beautiful. There were assembled about four hundred Kentuckians in the Old House of Representatives. The statues veiled with American flags were in their permanent places of prominence. After the invocation given by Rev. James Shera Montgomery, chaplain of the House of Representatives, and "My Old Kentucky Home" sung by Mrs. Kincheloe, Professor Frank L. McVey, as chairman of the statue committee, gave an address. He spoke of the glorious careers of the two Kentuckians, of their gifts to humanity, one in the field of political ideas, the other in medicine. I was deeply touched that in concluding his remarks he spoke of the spirit in which I had been prompted to make the gift, and expressed in glowing words the appreciation of Kentucky.

The statues were then unveiled by my two granddaughters, Miss Ann Burnham and Miss Nancy Burnham. It was indeed a dramatic moment when the draped flags parted to disclose the beautiful statues, and the assembled Kentuckians broke into applause at the sight of the two dignified figures. After short addresses from the Kentucky senators, and musical selections by the United States Army Band, the colorful ceremony closed with a benediction.

JOINT HOUSE RESOLUTION

WHEREAS, Mr. Isaac W. Bernheim, for more than sixty years a resident of this commonwealth, has generously offered to donate to the State of Kentucky two statues of Kentucky's sons to be placed in Statuary Hall, Washington, and

WHEREAS, It is the desire of the legislature of Kentucky to accept with gratitude the offer so graciously made, therefore,

BE IT RESOLVED BY THE HOUSE OF REPRESENTATIVES OF THE COMMONWEALTH OF KENTUCKY, THE SENATE CONCURRING:

First — The offer of Mr. Isaac W. Bernheim to give on behalf of the State of Kentucky two statues to be placed in Statuary Hall in Washington, D. C., in accordance with the laws of the United States governing such statues, is hereby accepted with the thanks of this commonwealth.

Second — A commission consisting of the President of the University of Kentucky, the President of the University of Louisville, and the President of Berea College, is hereby created, the duties of said commission to be to select after proper investigation those two persons who have been citizens of this commonwealth, who shall best represent it in Statuary Hall, and name those persons as subjects of said statues, and said commission is further authorized to make the necessary arrangements for the formal gift of said statues to the United States and the acceptance thereof by the Congress of the United States, or the proper officials thereof.

Third — This resolution, duly certified, shall be sent to Mr. Isaac W. Bernheim as a formal expression of the appreciation of the General Assembly of the Commonwealth of Kentucky of his generosity.

(Signed) CHAS. J. HOWES,
Chief Clerk of the House of Representatives
March 16, 1926

MY EIGHTIETH BIRTHDAY

"What makes old age so sad is not that our joys but that our hopes cease."

— JEAN PAUL RICHTER

Eighty years old! I thought those words over and over again in November, 1928, as the train bore Mrs. Bernheim and me from our summer home in Denver to Cincinnati. In retrospect I reviewed my life, realizing the struggles, the pleasures, the sorrows and the achievements that had been mine. I knew that in Cincinnati plans had been completed for the celebration on November fourth of my anniversary, that arrangements had been made for the reception that was planned, and that a banquet would follow.

It was with a mellowed heart that I looked forward to the meeting with my children and grandchildren, their husbands and wives, and my friends. At eighty years of age one will naturally take an inventory of one's life. There is an inclination to look placidly into the future, and to wonder if another birthday will be noted. I believe at this time one realizes with awe that the years to come will be very few. I know such thoughts were in my mind, but I can truthfully say that they were only passing with me. I was in the best of health, happy in heart, contented in mind. In a study of my life I felt with satisfaction and without egotism that when the final end came I would count as one who had been faithful to the trust Providence had placed with me.

The journey from Denver to Cincinnati, however, was not all spent in personal review of my life, for more was I anticipating the reunion with those nearest and dearest to me. Upon arrival in Cincinnati I was greeted by members of my family and on reaching my hotel found that the thoughtfulness of my daughters had provided everything in readiness for me.

Words would be futile in an attempt to describe my feelings when Mrs. Bernheim and I on the morning of my birthday stepped into the drawing rooms reserved for the welcoming of friends.

From early in the morning, flowers, books, telegrams, letters had flowed in until it seemed that the rooms would be inundated. The floral flood continued until noon. Through the help of many willing hands some semblance of order was obtained, and by the afternoon the two reception rooms were banked with beautiful roses, chrysanthemums, carnations and lilies, converting them into veritable bowers.

It was amid these tokens of esteem and affection that among the first friends to arrive I received a delegation from the Union of American Hebrew Congregations. Mr. Charles Shohl, acting as chairman, presented a beautiful basket of flowers in appreciation of the services I had rendered both the Congregation and the Union. In speaking for his fellow delegates, Mr. Shohl said:

"WE ARE HERE AS A COMMITTEE, APPOINTED BY MR. LUDWIG VOGELSTEIN, CHAIRMAN OF THE EXECUTIVE BOARD OF THE UNION OF AMERICAN HEBREW CONGREGATIONS, TO TENDER YOU THE CONGRATULATIONS OF THE UNION ON YOUR EIGHTIETH BIRTHDAY ANNIVERSARY.

"YOU HAVE REASON TO BE PROUD AND HAPPY OF YOUR LIFE'S RECORD. FROM YOUR EARLY MANHOOD YOU HAVE NOT ONLY BEEN A LEADER IN THE COMMERCIAL WALKS OF LIFE, BUT ALSO A WORTHY CITIZEN OF THE COMMUNITY IN WHICH YOU LIVED, A LIBERAL SUPPORTER OF EVERY WORTHY CHARITY AND A MAN RESPECTED BY ALL WHO KNEW YOU. IN ADDITION TO OUR CONGRATULATIONS WE WANT TO EXPRESS OUR APPRECIATION FOR WHAT YOU HAVE BEEN AND WHAT YOU HAVE DONE FOR THE UNION OF AMERICAN HEBREW CONGREGATIONS.

"OUR PRESENT LIBRARY BUILDING, DONATED BY YOU IS AN EVIDENCE OF YOUR EXTREME LIBERALITY, AND AS VICE-PRESIDENT OF THE UNION AND A MEMBER OF ITS EXECUTIVE BOARD, YOU HAVE ALWAYS SHOWN A KEEN INTEREST IN AND HAVE BEEN OF GREAT SERVICE TO OUR CAUSE.

"ALTHOUGH ADVANCED IN YEARS, YOU STILL BY THE GRACE OF

GOD POSSESS THE FULL VIGOR OF MANHOOD.

"MAY MANY ADDITIONAL YEARS BE GRANTED TO YOU AND MAY YOU LIVE TO ENJOY IN HEALTH AND HAPPINESS MANY ANNIVERSARIES OF YOUR BIRTHDAY SURROUNDED BY YOUR DEAR ONES AND THE MANY WHO RESPECT AND LOVE YOU,

"MAY GOD GUARD AND BLESS YOU, IS OUR HOPE, OUR WISH, OUR PRAYER."

I was deeply touched by his words and the spirit in which the flowers were given to me. I responded feelingly and thanked the gentlemen for the honor paid me, and for their gift. Just as the members of the delegation were shaking hands with me, Dr. S. Oko, Librarian of the Hebrew Union College, joined the group to extend his personal congratulations. The presence of Dr. Oko, the warm friendliness of all the delegates from the Union, prompted me to announce that I would contribute $25,000 to the building fund for the new library, the old one which I had given now being too small for the ever-increasing collection. This evidence of my further interest in the Union was the occasion for hearty applause. I smiled at the enthusiasm of my friends, and told them that I had considered Providence had been extremely kind to me, far beyond by deserts, and that I thought that although anniversaries were often celebrated by receiving gifts, I had decided that I would derive greater pleasure from giving something away. In making the promise of these funds to Dr. Oko I added my hopes for the continued success and usefulness of the library.

All afternoon friends thronged in to congratulate me and many were the happy reunions with associates whom I had not seen for many years.

That evening at seven-thirty, at the Losantiville Country Club, a sumptuous birthday dinner was held. I sat at the head of the board. Around the beautifully decorated table, sparkling with silver and glass reflecting the festive spirit of the occasion, were gathered my wife, my children and grandchildren, my sister and other members of the family. It was a proud moment for me as I looked upon my descendants, and I thought: "They are a fine looking lot."

Trained as I am to be guided by my head rather than by my heart, and to withstand sentiment, I could not resist a feeling of emotion and fulfillment at this moment, for in a measure this anniversary was the culmination of my career. I had long been thought of and recognized as a pioneer, and whilst I had created a business and built a fortune, the results of my life were now before me as a far greater achievement. I had become an ancestor, the head of a line, and had the rare satisfaction of seeing my scions worthy men and women, all ably taking their places in the world.

Throughout the dinner as occasion offered and conversation prompted, the guests rose to pay me eloquent tributes of affection and respect, and very often my heart beat fast, and tears welled to my eyes in my deep appreciation of their commendation.

Dr. Bertram Bernheim, my son, acting as impromptu toastmaster, paid me the compliment of saying that he thought me the most interesting man he had ever known.

Mr. Lewis Cole, my nephew, who for years had been closely associated with me in business, expressed his debt of gratitude for the training and assistance I had given him and asserted that without me he could never have achieved the success that was his.

My only sister, Mrs. Sara W. Cole, reminded us all of our origins. She grew reminiscent and spoke of the childhood of ourselves, contrasting the simple life in a German village with the complex life in urban America today. She spoke of incidents dear to us both, things which had happened in those faraway times that had become with the passage of years, but dim, fond memories.

Mrs. Bertram Bernheim, introducing a vein of humor, read a witty account of my activities, and cleverly wove into her speech references to many of my pet interests and hobbies.

Rabbi William Fineshriber was then called upon to offer a toast to my health. I think I can do no better than quote his words.

"This occasion is a very beautiful and rare opportunity to pay homage to a man who by dint of his own unaided efforts, fought his way up in this country from peddler to successful man of affairs. I want to remind the children and grandchildren of Mr. Bernheim that they cannot conceive of the hardships that he had endured during the early years. It was this very hardship, probably, which

TOUGHENED HIS MORAL FIBRE TO SUCH AN EXTENT THAT HE WAS ENABLED TO WITHSTAND THE RAVAGES OF TIME AND CIRCUMSTANCE. THOSE EXPERIENCES MAY HAVE HARDENED HIM A BIT BUT LOOKING BACK AT IT NOW OVER A PERIOD OF MANY YEARS, EVEN HIS KNOWN SEVERITY HAS PROVED USEFUL AND SALUTARY. MR. BERNHEIM IS AN UNUSUAL BLEND OF IDEALISM AND PRACTICALITY. HIS FEET HAVE ALWAYS BEEN PLANTED FIRMLY ON THE GROUND, BUT HIS EYES HAVE ALWAYS BEEN DIRECTED TOWARDS THE HEAVENS. IT IS VERY UNCOMMON FOR A MAN CIRCUMSTANCED AS HE HAS BEEN TO DEVOTE SO MUCH OF HIS VALUABLE TIME TO EDUCATION, PHILANTHROPIC AND CULTURAL EFFORTS, BUT IN ALL THESE THINGS MR. BERNHEIM HAS BEEN PREEMINENTLY USEFUL. WE CAN HOPE THAT, DESPITE HIS EIGHTY YEARS, MR. BERNHEIM WILL ENTER UPON A PERIOD OF SERENE ACTIVITY, AND WILL BECOME INCREASINGLY USEFUL TO HIS RELIGION AND HIS COUNTRY.

"ESSENTIALLY RELIGIOUS HE HAS ALWAYS BEEN, AND ONE OF THE OUTSTANDING CHARACTERISTICS OF HIS PERSONALITY, WHICH IS SO RICH AND MANY SIDED, HAS BEEN THIS DEVOTION TO RELIGIOUS LIFE. HE HAS ALWAYS TAKEN THIS RELIGION SERIOUSLY, AND HAS FOUGHT A WHOLE LIFETIME AGAINST WHAT HE BELIEVED TO BE INSINCERITY, COWARDICE, AND THE OTHER VICES THAT SO FREQUENTLY ENCUMBER RELIGIOUS ORGANIZATIONS."

Dr. Fineshriber then proposed a standing toast "in honor of the youthful octogenarian."

As I stood responding to the toast I felt so vital, so full of energy, that I was encouraged to tell them all to hope that there would be many more anniversaries, each one as happy and as colorful as this one. Life still had its interest for me, and my heart was filled with gratitude as the assembled company prayed that I would have the strength to bring to completion the philanthropic objects so dear to me.

I then turned to my children and spoke frankly and sincerely to them. I told my guests that even though they had spoken of my youth and vitality, I was not deceiving myself. I felt strong and well, but I realized that I was eighty years old. I said in part:

"Bernheim Luck" has become a maxim in my branch of the family, because on many occasions Providence seemed to be partial to me, and in its mysterious influence showed me the way not only to happiness and to success, but frequently prevented developments which would have led to disaster. Nothing convinces me more of God's beneficent continued favor than the fact that I am standing here in my eightieth year, still going strong and in possession of my faculties, somewhat dulled, but not seriously impaired.

"It is indeed a God-given privilege, one for which I thank Him daily. Let me confess, right here and now, I have not for-gotten how to pray, and to receive spiritual strength through it today as I did in my early years.

"In periods of reflection, one wonders how the world will look fifty years hence, and here am I standing before you with a well-defined personal knowledge of what the world did look like seventy and five years ago, and longer, because as a boy I was in intimate touch with men whose birth dated back to the latter part of the eighteenth century, say, almost one hundred and fifty years ago.

"I learned my lessons by the dim light of a candle, my parents owned the first coal oil lamp which was used in our village. It hung from a beam in the ceiling of our home in Schmieheim, spreading a light so brilliant as to astonish all of our neighbors. My grandfather on my father's side, a hard-working abstemious man, lived through the period of the French Revolution and served, so it was reported, as a soldier under Napoleon the First.

"My father, half free man, half slave, was one of the largest taxpayers in Schmieheim, but he was not allowed to vote. He served in the army but was not allowed to advance to the rank of corporal. And here I see before me a lot of people happy in the enjoyment of the privileges of a contented and comfortable life. Allow me once more to dwell on the fact that it was a kind Providence which directed me to these friendly shores where every man may sit under his own vine and fig tree, and no one to make him afraid.

"I, THE PIONEER, WAS INSTRUMENTAL IN BRINGING ABOUT THE TRANSFER TO AMERICA WITH MONEY SAVED FROM MY SCANT EARNINGS, FIRST MY BROTHER BERNARD, AND SHORTLY THEREAFTER MY DEAR MOTHER, AND THE REMAINING MEMBERS OF MY FAMILY. I COUNT THESE AS EVIDENCE OF A DESTINY FORMED AND SHAPED BY PROVIDENCE.

"LATER IN MY LIFE I BECAME A CONVERT TO THE THEORY THAT EVERY MAN WHO HAS MET WITH MATERIAL SUCCESS MUST LOOK UPON HIMSELF AS AN INVESTMENT OF THE COMMUNITY, AND THAT IT IS HIS DUTY TO DECLARE SUCH DIVIDENDS IN SERVICE, AND IN OTHER THINGS OF VALUE IN RETURN FOR THE PROTECTION WHICH HE HAS RECEIVED, AND WHICH ENABLED HIM TO REACH SUCCESS.

"I AM SAYING IT IN MODESTY, EARLY IN MY LIFE AND LONG BEFORE I WAS LOOKED UPON AS A MAN OF WEALTH, TO BE CONCISE, WAY BACK IN EIGHTEEN HUNDRED AND EIGHTY-FOUR, DURING THE FLOOD IN PADUCAH I WAS PERMITTED TO FURNISH COAL TO THOSE WHO NEEDED IT TO KEEP THEM IN COMFORT, AND BREAD TO THE POOR UNTIL THEIR LABOR ENABLED THEM TO PROVIDE FOR THEMSELVES. I HAVE KEPT ON DECLARING DIVIDENDS FROM TIME TO TIME AND I THANK GOD THAT I AM ABLE TO STATE THAT I HAVE NOT FINISHED YET."

And now a moment full of sadness came as I asked my guests to stand in silence in memory of those loved ones who were no longer with us.

Although the hour was late, no one wished to be the first to break the family circle, we lingered on speaking of the days gone by, reviving scenes of childhood but at last time for departures came, and with fervent handshakes and warm salutations the party broke up.

MY DREAM

"In sleep, when fancy is let loose to play,
Our dreams repeat the wishes of the day."

— CLAUDIUS

DREAMS were mine in that far-off day in Germany, when as a boy I walked to school. They were with me when I was struggling upward in early life, when I emigrated to America, and when I tramped the country roads of Pennsylvania selling Yankee notions from farm to farm. My dreams remained with me as my business grew and expanded through the years. They ripened into maturity at my country home in Kentucky, and in never-to-be-forgotten walks and talks with my wife.

Our family of four boys and three girls were then in their teens, and as they approached man and womanhood they became the source of endless speculations. We built "Castles in Spain," most of which never materialized. Even at that time, during my many walks with Mrs. Bernheim in the woodland behind my home, I pondered on the uses to which my estate would be put when we were gone. The hope came to me then that in some way I could devote it to public use, and I planned, in my imagination, the creation of an Arboretum and Herbarium, the nucleus of which would be found in the three hundred acres of land surrounding my home.

The death of my dear wife on December 9, 1922, changed the entire course of my life. I was uprooted from Kentucky, and in ways too intimate for recital here, the immediate realization of my dream became impossible. However, my plans, though deferred, were not abandoned. The years passed, I took up the threads of life again, business interests claimed my time, and yet, in the back of my mind I still carried my dream. As my fortune increased it permitted me to think of the enterprise on a larger scale. At last, on May 10, 1929, the physical materialization of my dream was brought about in the incorporation of the Isaac W. Bernheim Foundation, and the acquisition of more than thirteen thousand acres of wild "Kentucky Knob" land situated within twenty-five miles of the city of Louisville — an estate exceeding twenty square miles admirably suited for my purpose.

For the first time I can now visualize the future and more complete fulfillment of my dreams, the full realization of which, in view of my age of eighty-one, I shall probably never see. But I am comforted in the firm belief that the good a man does lives after him. There are concrete examples of this today. I feel that because the men and women who now and in the future will have charge of the development of the foundation are people of vision, education and thought, the enterprise will be carried forward successfully.

And looking into the future, what do I see? A sanctuary for birds that fly and fowl that find their home on the water. The tract has its rippling streams, and lakes are easily made to lend not only a place for the water birds, but to enhance the beauty of the landscape. There will be foot and bridle paths and motor roads throughout the preserve, from which vistas of beauty will constantly unfold to the view. Predatory animals and venomous reptiles will not be tolerated within the estate, so that children and the most timid need have no fear.

Within the area controlled by the Foundation there will be large groups of forest trees indigenous to this continent, each group plainly and correctly marked and each carefully protected. I see in my mind's eye the Herbarium, of splendid proportions, sections of it scattered in different parts of the forest, wherein will grow every wildflower common to America. Beautiful shrubs of this and other countries will abound. In short, I visualize a natural park where there will be in profusion all things which gladden the soul and please the sight of man.

In suitable and convenient places throughout the forest there will be spaces for visitors to park their automobiles, and a landing field for aeroplanes. There will be carefully protected areas where the public may picnic, tennis courts, a golf course where people who are excluded from Country Clubs because of the expense may be able to enjoy the game. Ample provision will be made for playgrounds for children and centers where they may be instructed in the intimate nature lore of the vicinity. It is not intended, however, that the park will ever be used for camping purposes. The gates will be opened at sunrise and close with the setting of the sun.

No living creature will be put to death within the limits of the Bernheim Foundation, but vermin may be destroyed under the supervision of the heads of departments specifically charged with that task. Pistols, rifles and shotguns will be surrendered on entering the grounds, for it is my hope that as man will learn not to fear the beasts, so too, they will know man as a friend and not as a creature outvying the lowest beast in his destruction.

There will be no discussion of religion or politics, no trading or trafficking, only the sale of catalogues or guide books may be permitted within the confines of the park. No distinction will be shown between rich and poor, white or colored. Every respectable man, woman and child will be made welcome, and all will be treated with an equal consideration.

My vision embraces an edifice, beautiful in design, which will rise at some carefully selected high spot within the area. It may be of marble or of native stone. From an architectural point of view it will be imposing and graceful. Within it there will be an art gallery, worthy in every respect of the name, and one which in course of time, I trust, will become nationally known. Therein will be busts in bronze of men and women whose names have risen to places of distinctive honor in Kentucky — a lasting and ever-present inspiration to the youths who gaze upon their faces.

A museum of natural history containing specimens of every animal that is classified in the wild life of this hemisphere will be provided for. These will be displayed in their natural habitats, a method of exhibition which I much admire today in the Museum of Natural History in Denver, Colo., which I frequently visit. Connected with this building will be an auditorium dedicated to education in all branches.

The auditorium will have ample seating capacity and will be equipped with a stage arranged for dramatic entertainments. Upon the stage will be built a great organ to furnish music, and in addition there will be radio receiving apparatus, motion picture and television installations. I hope the fullest use will be made of the auditorium for the entertainment of the people, bringing them not only what is popular but what is best in all forms of culture.

I trust it will be found possible to bring to the Foundation eminent men and women to lecture on educational and instructive subjects, especially nature in all her phases.

As one stands at the entrance to this building he will see before him a magnificent fountain with statues at its base to represent in artistic form "Labor," "Liberty," "Loyalty," "Love," the four great graces of mankind. Around it will spread a beautiful park of two hundred acres exemplifying the landscape artist's highest art. Here, too, he will see a tall steel pole rearing its top far from the ground, and from it will float the American Flag, to be the center at intervals of patriotic gatherings, especially of children, who will be retold the story of liberty.

My dream embraces a broad boulevard lined with forest trees and shrubbery leading from the main road to the entrance of this wooded retreat, and sweeping in broad curves to the central administrative building.

To all I send the invitation to come from city, village, hamlet and farm, to re-create their lives in the enjoyment of nature and the many blessings she gives with open hand to those with understanding, in the park which I have dedicated to the use of the people, and which I hope will be kept forever free.

THE REFORM CHURCH OF AMERICAN ISRAELITES

AN ADDRESS DELIVERED BEFORE THE BIENNIAL MEETING OF THE UNION OF AMERICAN HEBREW CONGREGATIONS, BUFFALO, N.Y., MAY, 1921

GLADSTONE, the great English statesman, in one of his speeches, said:

"Censure and criticism never hurt anybody. If false, they can't hurt you unless you are wanting in manly character; and, if true, they show a man his weak points and forewarn him against failure and trouble."

I am addressing you in the Gladstonian sense, and I may frankly say that only after mature reflection could I make up my mind to appear before you. Men at my time of life, who have back of them long years of strenuous activity, generally seek repose and are disinclined to engage in movements calculated to interfere with their comfort or peace of mind.

I am not unmindful of the fact that I am going to discuss a subject which the layman of our faith has heretofore left to men who by education were supposed to be better equipped for the task. I consider this rather unfortunate, for in the last analysis religion and religious tendencies have their practical sides no less than their spiritual ones.

When the practical in religion fails at least in some aspects to square with the spiritual, there must of necessity arise conditions which make it difficult, if not impossible, for religion to properly function, and this very situation forces upon me the conviction that the solution on our part of the question of the observance of the Sabbath Day can no longer be evaded or delayed.

Our Reformed Congregations are divided on this vital principle and are acting independently of each other. This situation is intolerable and cannot endure.

A sect divided thusly is headed for dissolution. We must either retrace our steps or bravely move forward. To retrace our steps is unthinkable for reasons which are obvious. Conviction, no less than consistency, should compel us to declare officially that the observance of the Sabbath Day of the Decalogue has become an economic impossibility and is no longer binding on us.

To adhere to a skeleton day of rest such as is now the rule in our Reform temples, where we thank God for the blessings of the Sabbath Day and then immediately thereafter proceed to resume our daily vocations, lays us open, and justly so, to the charge that we are materialists and that we are sacrificing a basic religious command for material gain.

If the outside world is not to question our sincere devotion to our religious principles, we must be honest with our neighbors, with ourselves, and with our God.

The one day of rest in seven has gained and continues to gain greater recognition as civilization advances towards higher human ideals. It being essentially of Hebrew origin, the world looks askance at its desecration on the part of those who have been specifically charged "To remember the Sabbath and keep it holy," and will not condone the violation of the ancient Sabbath Day, nor will society tolerate a double standard in religion any more than it will tolerate a double standard of morality without exacting the price. The issue is squarely before our co-religionists. It must be met courageously—double dealing will not solve it to our satisfaction, nor to the satisfaction of our fellow citizens of other faiths.

As I understand the history of reform in Israel, it has been a process of disentangling the universal from the original national or Oriental, the essential from the non-essential, the permanent from the passing. The ultimate purpose of this process is to teach the nations of the world the pure doctrine of the One God, and whatever obscures that process must be discarded. We simplified our ritual and translated it into the vernacular, not only that modern Israel might understand and pray intelligently and sincerely, but that also all other devout seekers after truth might know that our religion is universal in its scope. We introduced family pews because we believe that women have the same rights and privileges that men have in the house of God; we pray with uncovered heads because that is the modern Occidental way of manifesting reverence in worship; we abolished certain superfluous holy days and prayers. In brief, we had the courage to break with the past for the sake of the present and the future.

But we have not finished our work of emancipating the true spirit of our faith. The evil in the heart of Israel is that we do not observe our weekly day of rest as a holy day. Practical experience tells us that we do not, and, humanly speaking, the masses of us cannot observe the Saturday as a day of rest and worship. So, weakly, we compromise by all of us resting on Sunday and a few of us worshiping on Saturday. This cannot but result in confusion — confusion in our spiritual lives and confusion for our children and in the minds of the larger world. What we need in the premises is the same high courage that our pioneers manifested — break with our weak-kneed truckling to mere tradition and boldly declare that American Israel will henceforth observe Sunday as its day of rest and worship. In God's eyes it is all one whether we meet together to worship Him on Sunday or Saturday.

Let us understand each other fully. I am referring in this address solely to the people comprising the Union of American Hebrew Congregations and all those liberal elements friendly to its cause. Orthodox or semi-Orthodox members of the faith are not and cannot be expected to be in sympathy with this momentous change. Their religious conceptions will have to undergo the same clarifying process as did ours,

Dr. Isaac M. Wise was a man of vision, of strength, of character, and endowed with all the elements necessary for successful leadership. It has been my privilege to sit at his feet and to listen to him while in the performance of his duties as preacher and lecturer. I discussed with him on occasions by correspondence subjects mutually interesting. His sturdy Americanism stood out as broadly as did his devotion to his faith and ardent love for his people. And let me go on record right here by asserting that Dr. Wise's efforts as leader and reformer could not have succeeded had his work not been heartily supported by that sturdy class of European emigrants who were as deeply wedded to our American institutions and ideals as was he.

Far be it from me to detract, or to becloud, or to minimize the momentous work of Dr. Wise, but truth impels me to repeat that this great Master-builder could not have accomplished his object in so comparatively short space of time had he not had at his ready command the material with which to construct what is now known as American Reform Israel. This force consisted largely of emigrants who came from western Europe. In the old home they were deprived of their civil rights. The law under which they lived demanded military service but did not accord them the privilege to serve as corporals. It forced them to pay taxes, but denied them the right to vote.

These earnest men providentially underwent a most uniform and peculiar system of "Amercanization." They came here blessed with a good constitution, simple habits, indomitable industry and boundless ambition. They learned the beauties and attractions of American institutions at first hand by becoming peddlers, and from that lowly station full of hardship and sacrifices they graduated into the higher class—the merchant.

I am almost tempted to speak of that period in the plural form, because I pride myself on having been a graduate of that severe school which forced its followers to carry heavy burdens on their backs over hills and dales, but happily this humble occupation had its compensations — it brought with it the opportunity to come in daily contact with an element differing immensely from the elements which were left behind in the old country, and which attracted them with irresistible force.

The charm of the simple country life, its religious liberty, its peace and contentment, its social ease, the prevailing absence of caste and aristocracy, the democratic spirit, in short America — "our America" — with its basic principles that "all men are born free and equal, and all entitled to life, liberty and the pursuit of happiness," fashioned these active minds in a surprisingly short length of time into devoted, patriotic citizens, thoroughly imbued with the value, the principles and responsibilities of American citizenship. These sturdy men, the emigrants of the time prior to 1870, scattered throughout the length and breadth of the United States, proved wherever they dwelled desirable, law-abiding citizens, always ready to assume and assuming their full share in the development of their country.

They formed the material with which Dr. Wise laid the foundation for our Union. It was distinctly American in work, deed, thought, act and effect. The great reformer himself, a devoted patriot, a lover of his adopted country and an admirer of its institutions, amalgamated these elements and formed them into the Union of American Hebrew Congregations, preceding this with the publication of the *American Israelite*. I quote this because "AMERICA" was always writ in large letters in the heart of this great man, no less than in the hearts of his humble followers.

Zionism, political and otherwise, of the imported or domestic brand, was not in Dr. Wise's time, nor is it now, a thing to our liking, nor can it ever receive our support. Here is our Palestine, and we know no other. It would be contrary to one of our outstanding qualities of warm-heartedness to waive aside those millions of unfortunate human beings who have suffered so universally, largely because of their being of the Hebrew faith. Living as they do in eastern Europe, in territories which were ravaged and overrun again and again by contending forces, crushed under foot by every invader, their homes destroyed, or their families outraged and their possessions swept away, their pitiful situation makes overwhelming claims upon us. Our helpful and willing hands will ever be outstretched to them, and if in their attempt to better their conditions and seek a place in the sun they decide to emigrate to Palestine or elsewhere, we shall give them our unstinted support; but not as nation builders — only as colonists in the same sense and under the same conditions as emigrants from other lands receive. The attempt to re-create at this time or at any time in the future a so-called "Jewish State" will never meet with our sanction, and we solemnly protest against the slightest imputation, no matter from what source that charge may emanate, that we or our children are anything but 100 percent Americans and ready in the future as we have in the past to defend our rightful possession with our lives. We will neither countenance nor tolerate a hyphenism thrust upon us by Zionists, which if allowed to go unchallenged is threatening to lead us into a danger zone of appalling dimensions. Immediate action is demanded. Zionism and Americanism are not now and never will be synonymous.

Merely by way of illustration I quote from the May number of the *World's Work*, most influential periodical of unquestioned liberal tendency, as follows:

"Americans see in the Zionistic movement a menace to American solidarity; for anything that tends to make any section of the population transfer a modicum of its allegiance, even a sentimental and religious allegiance, to foreign soil is an impediment to that undivided devotion which true Americanism demands. Americanism, after all, is a jealous mistress and can brook no rivals."

Zionists are not all of one shade. They differ in their aspirations, methods, and purposes, but they dwell with singular unanimity and special ardor in their official documents and their propaganda literature on the use of the word "Jew." In their hysterical appeals they play fast and loose with the term "Jewry," attempting thereby to create the impression that "Jewry" comprises all the Jews in the universe and forming, as it were, a separate entity, a State within a State, a closed corporation of impractical dreamers and foreign reactionaries.

It would be a waste of time, after what has been stated by me before, to deny the base and absolutely false assumption that the Zionists represent even an infinitesimal part of the members of the Union of American Hebrew Congregations. Confirming this assertion, I herewith declare my readiness to turn over to them, to their heirs and assigns forever, the exclusive use of the word "Jew" and the term "Jewry."

The use of the word "Jewry" has no right to exist in our country. It is as repugnant to us as would be the word "Methodistry" or "Baptistry." We are enjoying here in common with all sects the fullest measure of religious liberty, and I deny the right of any religious body to constitute itself into a combine that would attempt to raise a barrier between themselves and the rest of their fellow citizens.

Dr. Adolph Moses, my sainted friend and rabbi, who graced the pulpit of the Louisville Reform Congregation for nearly twenty-five years, expressed himself in one of his sermons advocating the abrogation of the word "Jew" as follows:

"Among the innumerable misfortunes which have befallen the Israelites since they ceased to form a state and a nation, one of the most fatal in its consequences is the name Judaism. In the mind of the Gentiles this name indissolubly associates our religion, which is universal in its deepest sources and universal in its scope and tendency, with the Jewish race, and thus stamps it as a tribal religion. Worse still, the Jews themselves, who have gradually come to call their religion Judaism, are most of them misled to believe that their faith is bound up together with the Jewish race, and that it is a 'religion for Jews alone and not for people of any other race or nationality'."

He, the valiant fighter and thinker, almost prophetically foresaw the unfortunate results of the use of the words "Jew" and "Judaism." He had the courage of his conviction by publicly expressing his condemnation. His addresses on "Yahvism" are classics, and I hope will in the fullness of time find a place as textbooks in our college.

I quote further from the address of this saintly man:

JOSEPHUS, ZEALOUS FOR THE GLORY OF HIS NATION, WISHED TO PROVE TO HIS PAGAN CONTEMPORARIES THAT THE JEWISH CONCEPTION OF GOD, OF THE SOUL, OF MORALITY, ENSHRINED IN A NOBLE LITERATURE, WERE IN MOST RESPECTS SUPERIOR TO THOSE OF HELLENISM. AND TO THE TOTALITY OF THEIR BELIEFS, MORAL COMMANDMENTS, RELIGIOUS PRACTICES AND CEREMONIAL INSTITUTIONS HE GAVE THE NAME JUDAISM. THE CHRISTIAN WRITERS EAGERLY SEIZED UPON THE NAME THUS FURNISHED THEM, IN ORDER TO DISTINGUISH CHRISTIANITY FROM THE MOTHER-RELIGION FROM WHICH IT HAD SPRUNG AND BECOME DIFFERENTIATED; THEY WERE THUS ENABLED TO DEMONSTRATE TO THE HEATHENS, WHO WERE SEEKING THE TRUE GOD, THAT FOR THEM TO EMBRACE THE RELIGION OF ISRAEL MEANT TO BECOME JEWS, MEMBERS OF THE HATED, DESPISED AND ALREADY PERSECUTED JEWISH RACE.

Not only a great and respected preacher, a contemporary and friend of Dr. Wise, but also a distinguished layman of our faith, has been outspoken in his condemnation of the use of the word "Jew" and the term "Judaism." I quote from his pamphlet, which only reached a very limited circulation:

"WHAT IS THERE, AFTER ALL, TO SANCTIFY THE WORD "JEW," WHICH IS THE SIMPLE ENGLISH RENDERING OF THE HEBREW WORD "YEHUDI!" WHAT IS THERE TO JUSTIFY THE CONTINUED USE BY US OF THIS WORD, WHICH IS MERELY A RACIAL AND GEOGRAPHICAL TERM TO WHICH, PROPERLY SPEAKING, ONLY JEWS WHO ARE LIVING

IN JUDEA, PALESTINE, HAVE A VALID CLAIM? WE DO KNOW THAT THE WORD "JEW" WHICH OF COURSE DOES NOT APPEAR IN ANY SACRED TEXT, IN THE COURSE OF CENTURIES HAS ACQUIRED A DETERIORATED SIGNIFICATION, AND MOREOVER HAS BECOME A TERM WHICH OUR ENEMIES AND DETRACTORS EMPLOY TO EXPRESS THEIR HATRED, PREJUDICE AND CONTEMPT FOR EVEN PIETISTIC RABBIS HAVE DECLARED, THE WORD "JEW" IN ITS GENERAL APPLICATION AND ACCEPTATION NO LONGER DENOTES A RELIGIOUS AND ETHICAL PLATFORM, BUT HAS DEGENERATED INTO A TERM OF REPROACH, OR HAS BECOME A MERE NICKNAME.

THEREFORE AS IT HAS NO RELIGIOUS SANCTITY, IS NOT OF OUR CREED OR OF OUR LAWS, AS OUR FAITH WOULD NOT BE AFFECTED BY SUBSTITUTING FOR IT SOME OTHER NAME, WHY RETAIN IT, WHEN BY A MERE CHANGE OF NAME WE CROWN THE REFORM MOVEMENT WHICH DEVELOPED IN THIS COUNTRY IN THE LAST CENTURY UNDER THE LEADERSHIP OF ISAAC M. WISE, AND ENTIRELY FREE OURSELVES FROM ALLIANCES, ATTITUDES AND MOVEMENTS WITH WHICH WE ARE WHOLLY OUT OF SYMPATHY AND AGAINST WHICH WE RESOLUTELY PROTEST?

A HUMILIATING FACT TO FURTHER SUPPORT THE SUPREME NECESSITY OF RIDDING OUR FAITH OF ITS PRESENT TITLE IS THE COARSE CORRUPTION OF THE WORD "JEW" INTO A STANDARDIZED DEFINITION TO SIGNIFY CRAFTINESS, GREED, USURY, CHEAT, AND A MOST DESPICABLE FORM OF LOW CUNNING.

THE CENTURY DICTIONARY (LATEST EDITION), AN UNIMPEACHABLE AUTHORITY, UNDER THE WORD "JEW," AFTER DEFINING IT AS SIGNIFYING A MEMBER OF THE JEWISH RELIGION AND RACE, GIVES THE FOLLOWING ADDITIONAL DEFINITIONS TO THE WORD: "A PERSON WHO SEEKS GAIN BY SORDID OR CRAFTY MEANS; A HARD-FISTED MONEY-LENDER, OR TRICKY DEALER; AN OPPROBRIOUS USE, AS 'HE IS A REGULAR JEW.'"

"1. TO OVERREACH; CHEAT; BEAT UNFAIRLY AT A BARGAIN; AS, TO JEW ONE OUT OF A DOLLAR.

2. TO PRACTICE ARTS OF OVERREACHING OR CHEATING IN TRADE."

THE STANDARD DICTIONARY OF THE ENGLISH LANGUAGE (LATEST EDITION), ACCEPTED AS AN AUTHORITY EQUAL TO THE CENTURY DICTIONARY, UNDER THE WORD "JEW," GIVES THE THIRD DEFINITION:

"3. A CRAFTY DEALER OR GRASPING MONEY-LENDER, ONE WHO DRIVES HARD BARGAINS."

THE SAME DICTIONARY ALSO GIVES THE FOLLOWING DEFINITION OF THE VERB "JEW":

"TO GET THE BETTER OF IN A BARGAIN; OVERREACH; REFERRING TO THE PROVERBIAL KEENNESS OF JEWISH TRADERS.

TO PRACTICE SHARP METHODS IN A TRADE SUCH AS ARE REGULARLY ASCRIBED TO JEWS — TO JEW DOWN, TO INDUCE BY CHAFFERING TO TAKE A LOWER PRICE."

THE FACT THAT THIS OPPROBRIOUS DEFINITION IS GIVEN PLACE IN THIS DICTIONARY GIVES ASSURANCE THAT THE WORD IS NEVER DESTINED TO ATTAIN A REPUTABLE STANDING.

ROGET'S THESAURUS, RECOGNIZED BY ALL ENGLISH SCHOLARS AND LINGUISTS AS THE STANDARD AUTHORITY ON SYNONYMS, UNDER THE WORD "JEW", GIVES IT THE FOLLOWING VARIED MEANINGS, AMONG OTHERS: CUNNING, EXTORTIONER, USURER, HARPY, MISER, ETC.

IT SHOULD NOT BE OVERLOOKED THAT THESE DEFINITIONS, FIXED BY THESE STANDARD AUTHORITIES, IMPLY THAT THE COARSE, VULGAR MEANING OF THE WORD IS DERIVED FROM THE CHARACTERISTICS OF THE PEOPLE THEMSELVES, THUS PLACING THE INDELIBLE SEAL OF OPPROBRIUM BY UNIVERSALLY ACCEPTED AUTHORITIES OF THE ENGLISH LANGUAGE ON THE WORD "JEW" WHETHER APPLIED TO THE PEOPLE, THE FAITH, OR TO THE CHARACTERISTICS OF THE SECT BEARING THAT NAME.

DOES NOT THIS SITUATION OF ITSELF, IRRESPECTIVE OF THE OTHER REASONS SET FORTH ABOVE, FORCE THE ENGLISH-SPEAKING MEMBERS OF OUR FAITH TO REBUKE THIS LINGUISTIC SLANDER BY DISCARDING AN APPELLATION WHICH OUR ENEMIES CORRUPTED INTO A TERM OF REPROACH, AND COMPEL US TO SUBSTITUTE FOR THAT TITLE SOME NAME WHICH WE OURSELVES MAY CHOOSE, WHICH WILL EXPRESS IN A PROPER WORD OUR BELIEF IN ONE GOD, THE CORNERSTONE OF OUR RELIGION?

If the use of the term "Jew and Judaism" is a reservoir from which is fed the perennial spring of hatred, malice and contempt, the selection of the names for our places of worship such as "temple," which is of Roman origin, or "synagogue," which is of Greek origin, has added no little to the ammunition of our detractors by strengthening their accusation that we are a foreign and indigestible entity of the people among whom we live.

Tradition and custom are of no value if they lead only to suffering and martyrdom, and it is this very plea which has heretofore been employed so persistently and effectively by our spiritual leaders, when efforts had been made to emancipate ourselves from forms which are of no religious importance and if persisted in will produce the deplorable results so noticeable among our co-religionists in Europe.

It is there where our faith, because of these archaic forms, is at its lowest ebb, and it is here in America where through the instrumentality of modern reform its influence has grown and where it has displayed a vitality and renaissance absolutely unknown anywhere in the civilized world. These results should and must stimulate us in efforts towards further emancipation from the thralldom of indefinable sentimentalities. It is high time that we courageously face these problems and honestly as well as sensibly find a solution. The word "synagogue" or "temple" has no religious meaning for us. They are of foreign origin and should and must give way to the simple name of "church," which in our country is known and understood to be a place of worship.

I would urge this assembly, as I did our rabbis at their conference in the summer of 1918, to rededicate our places of worship, wherever situated, as the "Reform Churches of American Israelites." They would then be promptly converted into an active and aggressive force, broad enough, and wide enough, and tolerant enough to admit all of our brethren and all others "who have seen the light" and are ready to enter its portals. It would confirm the prophetic promise, "Mine house shall be an house of prayer for all people."

I have already indicated the reasons why I believe the names of "Jew" and "Judaism" should be changed to those of Israel and Israelite. Not only our history, but our ritual sanctions it. The great slogan of our faith is not "Hear, O Jews, the Lord is Our God, the Lord is One," but "Hear, O Israel." We speak of the mission of Israel, the House of Israel, the Faith of Israel, and we are understood. Why, then, waste so much precious energy in trying to overcome the misunderstanding and the obloquy that the centuries have heaped upon the word "Jew"? Rather let us use that surplus energy in bringing the central truth of

Israel to the attention of the world. Let us actively fulfill our mission, and not waste ourselves by foolish and useless apologetics.

My suggestion, then, is that we proceed logically and practically to the formation of the Reform Church of American Israelites. Let us make solemn declaration that we continue the work of Isaac M. Wise and his courageous contemporaries. Let us convert into actuality our reiterated creed that we are a religious body. Let us demonstrate by every adequate means that we are Americans by nationality, that our longings are not for an Oriental Palestinian homeland, that our hearts are here, our homes are here — here in America. Let us consecrate ourselves anew to our God, on the day which we can wholeheartedly devote to Him. Let us have a genuine Sabbath Day, untouched by compromise or sophistry. Let us be known by the hallowed, historic name of Israel, and ours the REFORM CHURCH OF AMERICAN ISRAELITES.

The above address was violently attacked by many rabbis, however, the principles advanced and the changes advocated received the unqualified endorsement of thousands of liberal laymen from every part of the United States.

I had intended to organize these into an aggressive body, when death robbed me of my unforgettable wife, and unfitted me for the task.

American Israel can only reach its fullest fruition when the ancient Sabbath will have been shelved and Sunday universally adopted as the day of rest, and when it will have emancipated itself from all tribal forms and oriental ceremonies.

The failure of the Jewish rabbis relentlessly to modernize their creed and worship is driving liberal-minded Jews from all religion or into liberal non-Jewish cults.

Palestine is likely to become the theatre of a tragedy involving the Arab and the Zionist in ever-increasing violence. Reform Israelites throughout the world should steer clear of this iridescent dream and maintain untarnished the integrity of their citizenship in the country where they dwell, and where their families have struck root.

NOVEMBER, 1929.   I. W. B.

Isaac Wolfe Bernheim

A PERSONAL STUDY

THERE are men who go through life little understood by their friends, their associates, or even their families. They disclose one side of their nature, the other is so closely hidden that only occasional glimpses are seen. Life moves swiftly for the majority of us and we give only passing notice, frequently, to the varied characteristics of our most intimate friends.

Isaac Wolfe Bernheim is a striking example of the man with two divergent personalities. One he has made visible to the world, the other, while it has appeared many times, has been overshadowed. The side that the world has seen is so strong and dominant that many have been apt to believe it is his only one. Yet his munificence, his gifts and benefactions have made his name familiar in widely different spheres of human activity at home and abroad.

Possibly there are some of his friends, who, while aware of his philanthropies, have failed to realize that these could have come only from a heart that beat in unison with the cause of those less fortunate than himself. They have failed to take into consideration that he knew privation in his childhood and youth, and that these trials have made known to him the needs of those whom he has helped in the days of his affluence.

The writer has had an unusual opportunity over a number of years for an analytical and personal study of Mr. Bernheim. I have known him intimately, perhaps more intimately than many who have met him only in the contact of business or casually in social intercourse. Through the close relationship which it has been my privilege to enjoy I have been able to pierce behind the barriers of reserve and shyness that have made him to many people aloof and distant. I believe a sympathetic and comprehensive insight into his life and the character that underlies a cold exterior is necessary, and hence this sketch.

There must always have been something of leadership in Mr. Bernheim. As a little boy, a serious youngster trudging off to school

THE BERNHEIM MEMORIAL ADDITION TO THE JEWISH
HOSPITAL, LOUISVILLE, KENTUCKY, OPENED 1929

under the greatest of hardships, he formed his own conclusions about
the adults in the world, with the insight of a grown man. His eyes cast
forward, always forward. Work would ever be his god, a stern, stony
god who would sit hard upon him while he was dancing quadrilles
with the village girls in Pennsylvania. It would be reigning several
years later when, with the rather unquestionable evidence that one of
his children was to be born within the next few days, he set out on a
business trip in compliance with his unalterable schedule.

He was resolute about the importance of work, more than anything
else. His working hours were long. His evening meal was invariably
one hour later than that of the rest of the community. Clocks, whistles,
sirens meant only annoyance when he was in the midst of business
problems. His office force stayed on with him, and although they
could not appreciate it then, they were never to regret it.

Despite this whole-hearted devotion to his business, Mr. Bernheim
did not lack time for an intelligent interest in outside affairs. A
charming conversationalist he could speak with the assurance of the

well informed and he fearlessly held his opinions. A typical instance of this occurred when the location of the new Jewish temple in Louisville, Ky., was under consideration. He was not afraid to be absolutely alone and to defy the entire congregation with his suggestion that the building should be erected where the more progressive enterprises of the city seemed to be moving. His opinion was overruled, the temple was erected in a locality which he condemned, and the congregation has never ceased to be sorry for it.

This courageous man is small physically. He is short in stature and unimpressive until he speaks, or one can see his penetrating eyes. It has never occurred to him to be afraid. While more than one man, acquaintance, employee, even son, were intimidated in the presence of his searching eyes and the swiftness of his catechism, there was compensation in his understanding and sudden sympathy. In the clear light of his logic he could discern the most minute of things. Whatever subject he became interested in he pursued down to its smallest detail, allowing no shortcuts, or half-digested theories to mislead him. Dishonesty never lifted its head within the precincts of his own integrity. Men in his employ stole from him, and he pretended to overlook their back slidings, sometimes even twice. Outsiders were apt to misjudge him, "impatient" they said of him, because he did not smother his thoughts or his opinions in quiet submission.

It is not difficult to find the sources of the independence of thought which sets Mr. Bernheim apart from the majority of men. His mother displayed it when she was brave enough to discard the old and hideous Jewish custom of concealing the hair upon entering the married state. It was from this dainty, attractive, wholly feminine lady that he inherited many of his most vigorous and powerful characteristics, and his numerous capabilities. But he was fortunate in both his parents. They were notably superior people. His father, Leon Solomon Bernheim, a prosperous merchant in the little village of Schmieheim, remained a bachelor, resisting the charms of the eligible maidens of the neighboring towns, for many years. He bided his time and choice until his thirty-sixth year. It is not to be wondered that his consequent selection was worthy of so discriminating an eye. Fanny Dreyfuss, daughter of Rabbi Moses Baer Dreyfuss, of a nearby town, became his wife at eighteen years of age. Beautiful, intelligent and well educated, she held a no less significant place in her own field of desirability. What a privilege to be born of these two talented individuals! It was by no means the least judicious action of a long career marked for its prudence that young Isaac managed to acquire such heredity.

Mr. Bernheim was a child of seven when his father was stricken with a fatal disease and died in his forty-eighth year. Within that brief span of his childhood he learned to cherish a respect and an admiration for that kindly, big-hearted man well beloved in the entire community for his charity. "One-tenth of whatever he raised in his fields, and one-tenth of his profits from other pursuits conscientiously went to the poor," his son remembers, and now closely allied, a generation later is the son's generous thought for the needy.

As early as 1884, when he was still a young man, father of a growing family and in modest circumstances, he furnished the poor of the town in which he lived with their winter supply of coal. The gift has never been withdrawn.

Within two years of his father's death Mr. Bernheim's mother married again. Child though he was, he became keenly conscious of his stepfather's shortcomings. The same shrewd practicality that has ever been uppermost in his mind was already making the little boy aware of the mismanagement of his father's estate.

When any other lad of ten would have had his pockets filled with marbles, and his mind stuffed with a little boy's nonsense, he was contemplating the wreck of his parent's fortune, criticizing the mistakes made by his mother's talented but unsuccessful husband. On those long walks which he was taking to school at Ettenheim, four miles away from his home, in all kinds of weather, and while suffering every inconvenience, he had plenty of time to think. It is almost impossible for any of us, these days, to imagine a youngster for whom underwear was a luxury too dear to be afforded, and who did not possess an overcoat, trudging off to a school where he was not compelled to go,

What such a boy was made of is easy to see. As he himself most vividly recalls, he was far from angelic. He did not persuade his small legs with arguments as to the high moral purpose of such hardship. He did not go because he should go. Without a doubt, he had figured in his hard little head the advantage of an education even at the expense of three winters of icy mornings.

At a time when he was nothing but a child he had decided there was something within him that set him aside from his schoolmates, and he saw no reason why he should associate with the rough and carefree lads that surrounded him. In his yet underwear-less and coatless state he was already confident of his ability. He selected his friends carefully and with discrimination.

Mr. Bernheim was thirteen years old at the time of the dramatic liberation of the Jews in Germany, an Act which opened the gates of many of the cities to the Jews in Germany, heretofore restricted to designated villages and towns. His family joined the great procession of their co-religionists moving towards the once forbidden cities. Gathering together what little remained of the family fortune, they took up residence in Freiburg and here for three years the boy, Isaac, was attached to a commercial house. An apprenticeship, they called it in those days when mere children worked from morning to night and received no compensation with the exception of the little practical knowledge they might assimilate.

With what eagerness and fortitude he approached that first meager job! But, however, no clerk who immediately realized the limitations of his opportunities in his position and who at once sought better connections, would long remain a clerk. He obtained more advantageous employment and was increasingly successful, when suddenly that Daemonic being inside of him lifted its head at an extremely opportune moment and sang attractively of America. Words like Opportunity and Freedom were synonyms for America then. Healthy, prosperous individuals were returning to the Old Country for visits.

America in 1867 lacked nearly everything but a golden reputation. Her communication with the outside world was by tremendous oceans, crossing the Atlantic in those days was an uncomfortable experience of more than two weeks. Voyagers and settlers on their return to Europe had plenty of time to forget its crudeness, the newness, and the homeliness of much of America.

The enthusiastic conversation of an uncle from New York added an additional spur. His glowing tales of success in the new country were enough to quicken the inner spirit and start the boy on his odyssey.

The young man left behind him family, friends and the certitude of a position, as he emigrated to America.

Mr. Bernheim landed in New York in the spring of the year 1867. He was eighteen, reasonably certain of his abilities and despite the lack of more than four American dollars in his pocket, confident of his power to wrest from the future his share of fortune. Alas, for the dreams of youth! At eighteen it is so easy to have one's air castles toppled over in an instant. At the time of his arrival in America the country had by no means recovered from the ill effects of the Civil War. All around huge fortunes were tumbling, panic prevailed. The uncle who had so breezily outlined his future, was struggling to evade an imminent financial failure. The fall of Isaac's dreams was as a drop of water in the storm of disaster which was blighting the commercial life of the country.

His relative could give him no employment. Looking for a job in New York was a meaningless thing for there was no work to be had. This for a young adventurer who had deserted security in Germany, was a severe blow. But he was courageously cheerful and willing to do anything. Friends of his uncle offered him some goods to peddle in Pennsylvania. He shouldered his small pack of then so-called Yankee notions and set off to overcome the well-developed thrift of the Dutch housewives.

Coal dust was not hovering so thickly over Pennsylvania in the '60s as now. The hills and valleys of that beautiful state were then basking in the quiet life of a primitive Arcadia. Cornhusking parties and barn dances were the fashion on a countryside where in later years even the wildflowers were destined to suffer from the grime that years of industrialization had brought.

The poetry in the heart of the young German merchant rhymed with the charm of the people and a country brand new. Their hospitality appealed to him. Not unhandsome, with a noticeable personality and dignity, he was accepted into the social life of the villages. He enjoyed dancing, knew the intricacies of the waltz, and became a favorite with the young ladies. On through that first long, cold winter he traveled from village to village, taking life as it came, evading the crude pleasures of the men, saving money, improving his English, and learning to become one of the people. All seemed to be going well, when the poor old horse, which he had lately acquired and which represented half of his worldly goods, died.

The financial returns of the winter were almost negligible, but the young immigrant had gained a gold mine in experience. He was beginning to know the life and the people. The generous hospitality of the inhabitants in the villages where he peddled his wares, and he has never forgotten it, opened wide the opportunities for a share in their lives.

With the loss of half of his capital came the Spring. He sold what was left of his small stock and went further west to Paducah in Kentucky, whence his New York relatives had drifted by this time. The Kentucky town was, and still is, an exceptional place. It may look like any other town, its houses are set far back from shady streets, the majority of the shops are in the two-storied buildings which housed the very same conservative businesses in decades past, but the spirit of old and respectable aristocracy breathes quietly in the dignified homes of fifty years ago. Across the river in Illinois inheritance of prestige is little known or cared about, but Paducah preserves the importance of its old families.

Paducah sixty years ago was a village of four thousand inhabitants. Even the "old families" were quite youthful then. Everyone knew everyone else with that delightful intimacy which is at once so inviting and yet disquieting to the stranger. Into this closely knit Southern community came the somewhat rumpled Isaac, in his threadbare city clothes. At once in this environment where friendship constituted business he felt the handicap of being an outsider.

It was this, perhaps, that later formed for Mr. Bernheim one of his firmest principles: "Build friendship on trade, not trade on friendship." Only a few years were required to prove that he was right.

After a short interval spent in clerking in a store, the young man accepted a position with a wholesale liquor firm and gradually he began to count himself as one of the community.

The girl Mr. Bernheim was to marry was made of lavender and old lace. She lived in the center of a charmed circle of loveliness all her own, and from the moment that he came within the radius of her influence he remained enchanted. Amanda Uri was the only woman whom he ever loved. She was the most sought-after young lady in the little social set of Paducah, and never was a man so wholly lost in admiration as was Isaac. The '70s were buggy-riding days. With pomp and seriousness the young couple drove away after dinner each Sunday afternoon. They were, of course, betrothed. After a long engagement they were married, when "Mandy" was but twenty and "Ike" had reached his twenty-sixth year. For four years Miss Uri had been the head of a motherless household, and straightway from the ceremony at the temple the couple hastened to the little house where "Mandy's" three small orphaned sisters were waiting to be put to bed.

In temperament and interests there were never two people so widely apart, yet their diverse personalities complemented one another. They were entirely happy. An angelic disposition and a domineering one combined to produce children who are gracious modifications of them both. Amanda was regal. Although quiet and unassuming, with an unvarying sweetness, she had a presence. In Paducah the people remember the stately lady who wore orchid-colored suits. Few women have been so universally loved. Her husband was devoutly in love with her always. She in turn adored his intellect, his knowledge, she was fascinated by the strength of his will. He dominated her completely and she liked it.

Nowhere does the character of Mr. Bernheim display itself so clearly as in his relationship with his wife. He loved her passionately, and yet so wedded was he to economy and rigid self-denial, that in later years when he was wealthy enough to afford every desire that she might express, and she was a charming woman he felt compelled to deny her a fur coat because he did not believe it to be a necessity, and could not bring himself to gratify a wish for something he considered a luxury, and which offended his principles.

The other individual who played an important part in his life was his brother, Bernard. Of the slow, easygoing type, genial, hearty and happy-go-lucky, he was the antithesis of Isaac.

Within a few months after Mr. Bernheim had accepted the position with the wholesale liquor firm, with his scant savings he brought his brother over from Germany. Before leaving Germany, Bernard had "mastered" the entire English language in a course of "six weeks of easy lessons." In spite of this handicap Isaac managed to transform him into an efficient bookkeeper in an American office, all in less time than three months.

LINCOLN MEMORIAL
LOUISVILLE, KENTUCKY, DEDICATED 1922

From the combination of these two men was to follow an ideal business partnership. Here was the essence of conservatism to be coupled with tumultuous daring, vision and courage. Alone, Bernard may have remained a small town merchant all his life; without his caution and deliberation, Isaac might have been a failure, the victim of his own impetuousness. Together they developed a business with representatives in every State of the Union, and abroad. Bernard could hardly be said to have exerted an influence on his brother two years his senior. No one could soften the hard shell of independence that surrounded Isaac. But, possibly, unconsciously, he contributed qualities which his brother lacked, and supplied just that amount of restraint needed to bring to earth the temperamental enthusiasm of his brother's genius.

The business of the two brothers prospered. They outgrew their connection with the liquor firm, and within three years had established themselves on their own account. In the back room of a small country store the two potential distillers and a Negro helper founded a "business." There were no regular hours, they ate and slept within calling distance of their customers. The fixtures in that establishment might have served easily as kitchen furniture, yet in a few years these two men would help to keep Kentucky's fame for her fine liquors, before the world.

The Paducah concern grew rapidly until that little town could no longer harbor it. It was Isaac W. Bernheim who sensed the possibilities of Louisville, a much larger city up the Ohio River. Bernard was dubious about the proposed change, but the business was transferred.

When Mr. Bernheim went to Louisville he was in the prime of life. He was forty, and twenty years of phenomenal success were behind him. The last of his seven children was born within the first year of his new residence. The next twenty years were busy, wonderful years. The youth who had arrived in America with four dollars in his pocket could now enjoy the pleasure of philanthropy, it was a giving of his own kind, and it was often misunderstood.

It is in the autumn of his life that Mr. Bernheim now has time to satisfy his long-held desire to participate in philanthropy. Until recent years he has been too much engrossed in his business affairs to do more than lay the foundations. But he has ever been a keen and accurate observer, storing up through the years impressions of human society now to receive the benefits of his generosity.

It is common for us to acclaim the greatness of the Soldier, the Statesman, the man of Science, but to the merchant, the man who furnishes the life blood of the community and in a large measure influences more than any other the destiny of the plain man, rarely is accorded the same recognition.

This is to be expected. A warrior, a scientist, an artist or a poet is judged in the main by his definite achievements. For the man of business there is no such exact measure of distinction, unless it be the amassing of a fortune, or in exceptional cases the founding of an industry.

It is therefore meet that a man who by his unaided efforts developed a large business, gave employment to thousands of men and women, accumulated riches, and then used them, not for his own aggrandizement or luxury, but for the good of his fellow man, should receive the appreciation due him. How frequently is this neglected. Compliments are apt to be considered flattery or mere persiflage, and those closest and having the best opportunity to form a true judgment too often are silent from the fear that the sentiment underlying their expressions will be misconstrued.

Those who have known Mr. Bernheim in his business life would say that his outstanding characteristic is his immense power for hard work. To me his finest quality is his unfailing pursuit of what seems to him right and just. Above all, the simplicity and clearness of vision which few carry beyond their earliest years stamps him as a man ever young.

Contempt for lowly beginnings, abhorrent as it is to any honest mind, is in his mind inconceivable. He reverences his mother and ever holds a deep love and devotion for the town which was his birthplace and the people who formed his character. Whilst never boastful, he always remembers to give credit to his immediate ancestors and does not forget that his race in their long sad history through the ages has given to him a priceless heritage.

Emancipated from superstition, divorced from separatism, broad and tolerant in his religious beliefs, he yet remains faithful to his people. Ever he has striven throughout his long life for reform and progress, and he is still active in movements which in his opinion will better the conditions of members of his faith. He visions the day when all traces of tribalism will disappear, and works for the time when his co-religionists in America will cease to look to the East, but will take their place in the Commonwealth of America as individuals free from prejudice and free also from the differentiation of outlook that has caused so much sorrow and hardship.

Beyond all else he is a Jew and has the Jewish faculty, so seldom seen among Gentiles, of being at once a man of dollars and a man of dreams.

The virility of his practicality is almost overpowering, His idealism and the dreams he envisions from afar are hidden beneath a stoicism and rigid discipline — too often mistaken for selfishness by the undiscerning. He combines to a most unusual degree the pragmatist and the idealist.

In matters of living, of questions as to immortality, he maintains an open mind. He holds mere speculation in open scorn. In his youth and middle age he sought in the Prophets the solid foundation on which to found his moral creed. From them he learned the wisdom of the good life. He came to know the lesson of experience not to trust to the crowd, not to be afraid to stand alone, to be lonely; to withstand with courage the damning opposition of men who did not agree with him. He expects little of life, and sees the folly of pursuing that chimera happiness, but do his duty he must. Gratitude he does not count upon, knowing the failings of the human race. Sensitive he is to slights, especially to thoughtless discourtesy, but never holds a grudge against any man, ever willing to let bygones be bygones.

Many opportunities were given to him to appear in public, but he avoided self-advertisement. The usual commonplace rounds of social life held no attractions for him. The cultivation of a few friends and devout love of his home and the country in which his manhood has been spent fills his hours outside of his business and philanthropic activities.

You who read will think, perhaps, this is but one side of his character. Are there no faults, no shortcomings? Have we not all our peculiarities, our idiosyncrasies? Some have made comment on his high temper, his impatience. His frankness, unconsciously indifferent to the sensibilities of others, gave offence to many. His rigidity and autocratic bearing became his because he was schooled in the old German manner. His coldness covered a shyness which he knew if allowed to be visible would prevent him from achieving the objective at which he aimed.

It is difficult to separate the gold of a man from the failings with which we are so much more likely to be intimate. With what rapidity we are apt to recall all that seems to us detrimental. His good qualities will be better appreciated in the years to come when the projects of his foresight will have been in existence for a long time. The autocratic disposition of a man is not going to live, but the autocrat will! When his predictions for the future of his religion come true, when the institutions which he helped to found and endow rank high, then no one will remember that he, along with the rest of us, could lose his temper.

He saw the opportunity to organize Jewish youth in Louisville, he recognized the possibilities for widespread good in the Jewish Hospital of that city. Again and again he supported educational projects. He was particularly interested in the problems of his religion. From his early manhood a sponsor of Reform Judaism, he was always ready to take up the cudgels on behalf of progress. His suggestions were many times greeted with adverse criticism, he was frequently execrated, but he was never overlooked. He advocated the change of the name Jew to Israelite to remove the opprobrium attached to a title historically incorrect. He still works to make the Hebraic Sabbath coincide with the Sunday of the modern world. Often he has been laughed at, frowned upon, rarely applauded, but right or wrong his ideas are always important enough and presented with such vigor as to turn the intelligence of other men in his direction. He is never ignored.

Behind his gifts and benefactions there is a mind that is still clear cut, incisive. His charity is of the unique kind that analyzes itself lest by allowing sentiment to encroach, the real and ultimate good intended may be destroyed. Wherever he has lived we find evidence of his appreciation of the needs of others. The statues of Jefferson and Lincoln in Louisville, Ky., of Clay and McDowell, representing Kentucky in Statuary Hall in Washington, D.C., the Library Building of the Hebrew Union College, Cincinnati, Ohio, the Young Men's Hebrew Association of Kentucky, the Orphan Society, and Old Men's Home in Germany, and now the Bernheim Foundation, together with his many acts of individual helpfulness, will continue to pay eloquent tribute to Mr. Bernheim in the years when he is no longer with us.

C. K.